Sustainability in Accounting Education

T0292905

Accounting sustainably involves accounting for and to the natural environment, and accounting for and to society, including groups currently oppressed or disadvantaged by unsustainable processes and practices. This book creates a compelling case for the inclusion of sustainability at the heart of accounting educational programmes, offering critical lessons and identifying risks to avoid when designing accounting programmes and courses. Accounting sustainability has moved from the side-lines of policy discourses, accounting institutions, professional accounting practices, and research activities into the mainstream. The chapters in this book engage in a critical dialogue to facilitate change in accounting education for sustainability. They dispel the myth that accounting for sustainability is an oxymoron, bad for business, unrelated to practice, or contrary to professional accounting bodies' accreditation requirements.

This book was originally published as a special issue of *Accounting Education: an international journal*.

Maria Cadiz Dyball is Associate Professor of Accounting at Macquarie University, Australia. She has diverse research interests that explore differences and shifts in philosophies and traditions and how these are mediated through, and reflected in, accounting professionalisation projects, practices, and education. Professor Dyball has published widely in top-tier academic and professional journals and her research is supported by external, competitive grants.

Ian Thomson is Professor of Accounting at the University of Strathclyde, UK. He has undertaken research into many different aspects of accounting and sustainability. These projects have included interdisciplinary studies on implementation of cleaner technology, establishing industrial ecologies, effective stakeholder engagement, risk governance in water and salmon farming, sustainable development indicators, government policy-making, external accounting, and accounting education. In 2012, he was elected Convener of the governing council of the Centre for Social and Environmental Accounting Research.

Richard M.S. Wilson is Emeritus Professor of Business Administration and Financial Management at Loughborough University, UK. He has devoted his career to boundary-spanning (e.g. as practitioner and professor, across disciplines, and in different jurisdictions). For 40 years he has been active nationally and internationally in educational policy-making on the interface of accounting education and training; has worked in more than a dozen countries; has published widely; is the founding Editor of *Accounting Education: an international journal;* holds two Lifetime Achievement Awards (one specifically for his work on accounting education); and is an Academician of the Academy of Social Sciences.

Sustainability in Accounting Education

Edited by
**Maria Cadiz Dyball, Ian Thomson and
Richard M.S. Wilson**

Routledge
Taylor & Francis Group

LONDON AND NEW YORK

First published 2014
by Routledge
2 Park Square, Milton Park, Abingdon, Oxfordshire OX14 4RN

and by Routledge
711 Third Avenue, New York, NY 10017, USA

First issued in paperback 2016

Routledge is an imprint of the Taylor & Francis Group, an informa business

British Library Cataloguing in Publication Data
A catalogue record for this book is available from the British Library

ISBN 13: 978-1-138-19283-6 (pbk)
ISBN 13: 978-1-138-77973-0 (hbk)

Typeset in Times New Roman
by Taylor & Francis Books

Publisher's Note
The publisher accepts responsibility for any inconsistencies that may have arisen during the conversion of this book from journal articles to book chapters, namely the possible inclusion of journal terminology.

Disclaimer
Every effort has been made to contact copyright holders for their permission to reprint material in this book. The publishers would be grateful to hear from any copyright holder who is not here acknowledged and will undertake to rectify any errors or omissions in future editions of this book.

Contents

CONTENTS

Citation Information

The chapters in this book were originally published in *Accounting Education: an international journal*, volume 22, issue 4 (August 2013). When citing this material, please use the original page numbering for each article, as follows:

Guest Editorial
Sustainability and Accounting Education
Maria Cadiz Dyball and Ian Thomson
Accounting Education: an international journal, volume 22, issue 4
(August 2013) pp. 303–307

Chapter 1
Sustainability and Accounting Education: The Elephant in the Classroom
Rob Gray
Accounting Education: an international journal, volume 22, issue 4
(August 2013) pp. 308–332

Chapter 2
A Commentary on 'Sustainability and Accounting Education:
The Elephant in the Classroom'
Matias Laine
Accounting Education: an international journal, volume 22, issue 4
(August 2013) pp. 333–335

Chapter 3
'Utopia' and 'Passion': A Commentary on 'Sustainability and
Accounting Education: The Elephant in the Classroom'
Massimo Contrafatto
Accounting Education: an international journal, volume 22, issue 4
(August 2013) pp. 336–339

Chapter 4
Integrated Reporting: A Review of Developments and their
Implications for the Accounting Curriculum
Gareth Owen
Accounting Education: an international journal, volume 22, issue 4
(August 2013) pp. 340–356

Please direct any queries you may have about the citations to
clsuk.permissions@cengage.com

Notes on Contributors

Jane Andrew, The University of Sydney, Australia

Massimo Contrafatto, University of Bergamo, Italy

Carmen Correa Ruiz, Universidad Pablo de Olavide, Spain

Maria Cadiz Dyball, Macquarie University, Australia

Jeff Everett, York University, Canada

Rob Gray, University of St Andrews, UK

Nancy Kamp-Roelands, Ernst & Young, The Netherlands

Matias Laine, University of Tampere, Finland

Carlos Larrinaga, Universidad de Burgos, Spain

Ken McPhail, La Trobe University, Australia

Gareth Owen, The Association of Chartered Certified Accountants, UK

Karin Reinhard, Baden-Wuerttemberg Cooperative State University, Germany

Stefan Schaltegger, Leuphana University, Lüneburg, Germany

Ian Thomson, University of Strathclyde, Scotland, UK

Kai-Uwe Wellner, University of Applied Science, Germany

Richard M.S. Wilson, Loughborough University, UK

Monte Wynder, University of the Sunshine Coast, Australia

and eco-justice. For example, the authors discuss accounting education in the context of integrating real and present environmental dangers into accounting, how to account for human rights, challenges associated with rethinking the accounting infrastructure to produce effective accounting-sustainability reports, as well as critically questioning the dominant epistemological underpinning of accounting from a sustainability perspective.

Accounting education practices are recognised in all papers and Commentaries as having a constitutive role in creating socially and environmentally (ir)responsible accounting professionals and citizens. However, this constitutive role can be either positive or negative, depending on the nature of their educational experience. Transforming accounting educational practices requires a re-alignment of accounting curricula with high level sustainability programmatic discourses, and in how to deal with the immediate imperatives and contradictions we all face when making decisions. There is a need for both theoretical critique and exploration of how to make accounting for sustainability real in specific organisational contexts. Transforming accounting education along a sustainability trajectory requires changes at many levels, and the papers in this themed issue provide arguments and evidence for system-wide reforms. Moreover, it is also important to create 'learning spaces' in existing accounting classes, to make accounting for sustainability real at a micro-level (for example, in how to turn accounting numbers into evaluations of sustainable performance). Within the papers there is a strong message that changing our everyday educational practices in how we teach topics such as financial reporting, costing, auditing or performance measurement is as important as teaching critical thinking and reflection skills.

The papers, Commentaries and Rejoinders report on a pull for more sustainable accounting from the accounting profession and other institutions providing evidence of a strong demand to embed sustainability in accounting educational programmes. However, there are also arguments that it is not sufficient for accounting educators simply to respond to external demands for change. As accounting academics we have a responsibility to look beyond the current terrain of accounting sustainability hybrid practices to scope out future dangers and seek to shape and construct authentic sustainable accounting. A strong message from these papers is that our education programmes need to be critically engaged with sustainability accounting practices, confronting practice from a sustainability perspective to push our students, graduates, organisations, professional institutions, policy-makers and government institutions. We need to integrate key lessons from leading edge research into the intersection between accounting and sustainability concerns, proactively constructing curricula that will build the capacity of our students to act as sustainable accountants and citizens throughout their lives. It is not enough to respond to external demands: we, as academics, should welcome these developments from the profession, but in our privileged social role of the critic and conscience of society we should be active in shaping and constructing a sustainable future for accountants, accountancy and the planet.

This issue of *Accounting Education: an international journal* on sustainability in accounting education reports on how accounting educators have responded to the challenges articulated in the United Nations Decade of Education for Sustainable Development (2005–2014), which seeks to integrate the principles, values and practices of sustainable development into all aspects of education and learning at universities. This themed issue contains papers, Commentaries and Rejoinders that provide valuable insights into the design and delivery of accounting education that reflect different international contexts, current sustainability thinking and practices, whilst educating students to critically examine ways in which accounting thinking and practices have and could contribute to society's unsustainability.

The paper by Gray is a challenge to accounting educators to urgently address sustainability, which he refers to as the 'elephant in the classroom'. His contention is that in the context of accounting education, whilst most regard sustainability as being very important for accounting, we are choosing to ignore it. He represents a compelling case that sustainability, as the most critical problem facing mankind, cannot continue to be ignored, and offers an example of one undergraduate course that is explicitly designed to confront students with their/our unsustainability and on the changes necessary to stop our headlong pursuit to planetary destruction. Central to his argument is a need to authentically engage with and understand what 'sustainability' is in order that we can appropriately account for it and effectively educate our students. Much of the passion and intensity of this paper is reflected in the Commentaries by Laine and Contrafatto. They both provide support for the importance of building accounting education around a critical understanding of sustainability and also offer practical insights and reflections from their experiences in Finland and Italy, respectively, in educating students in how to account for sustainability and get a good night's sleep! (Professor Gray chose not to write a Rejoinder to these two Commentaries.)

Owen offers a valuable insider's insight into the motivations, challenges and benefits of the process of integrating sustainability into professional accounting curricula and assessments. In his paper he reports on a number of drivers of this change and the desire of the Association of Chartered Certified Accountants (ACCA) to contribute to providing professional accountants with the necessary competence and knowledge in order to drive sustainable organisational change, with particular reference to developments associated with Integrated Reporting. These have led to the synthesis of six key outcomes that should be included within a modern professional accounting curriculum and a discussion of future accounting curriculum development to ensure professional and university accounting qualifications remain fully aligned with integrated reporting requirements beyond 2012. Kamp-Roelands offers a number of valuable insights as both an academic and leading practitioner in the field of accounting for sustainability in the Netherlands, Europe and globally. These insights complement and support the initiatives reported on by Owen, but also offer some additional support for the demand from the profession for accountants with skills and competences in sustainability, as well as the need for accountancy to be re-centred around ethical concern rather than technical competence. Correa Ruiz provides a number of valuable comments and ideas from the perspectives of an accounting academic in Spain. Her Commentary can be seen as supporting the initiatives undertaken by ACCA, but also challenging them to go further. Whilst welcoming and recognising the progress made in their curricula, she points out some gaps between the wider sustainability discourses and the ACCA, and identifies areas for further engagement between academia and professional institutions.

Wynder, Wellner and Reinhard's paper reports on a study conducted in Germany and Australia that attempts to empirically investigate whether the rhetoric that many universities have integrated sustainability into their accounting curricula has had an impact on the understanding and competences of students and practitioners. The evidence from a series of evaluation tasks provides positive support that exposure to education in environmental management accounting meant that Australian and German third-year accounting students recognised lead performance indicators and penalised poor environmental performance, more than first-year students and experienced accounting controllers. This would suggest that accounting education has the potential to change students' perceptions of environmental problems and improve skills in measuring environmental performance.

Larrinaga concludes in his Commentary that this experiment provides interesting insights into the impact of education on students, but offers some additional ways of interpreting the findings. He offers some constructive challenges to the authors' dependence on the logic of the 'business case' and the value of applying a more critical perspective. One insight is that accounting educators perhaps assume that the business case for environmental change and protection is desirable and therefore educate students accordingly, but that the evidence in this paper could indicate that in most cases a business case for environmental protection does not emerge in practice. He also suggests that the findings in this paper are worthy of further research and encourages others to open up the education black box to understand how education can allow accountants and business managers to deal ethically with issues associated with sustainability. Schaltegger also engages constructively with the findings, and supports the positive impact that can arise by integrating sustainability and environmental management into accounting education. He argues that accounting education can be redesigned to support 'change agents for sustainability' in exploring possible solutions to environmental and social problems, in overcoming obstacles and, in particular, the value of case studies of organisations that have successfully implemented more sustainable business practices. However, similar to Larrinaga, he stressed the importance of the type of educational experiences in driving positive attitudes in students and argues for further research into what constitutes effective environmental and sustainable accounting educational programmes, as well as consideration of the organisational contexts in which they will work.

McPhail explores the challenges to the dominant ideology taught in business schools arising from the emerging discourse on business and human rights. He identifies that few, if any, business schools contain any systematic and critical discussion of human rights in their accounting and business curricula. He then presents and outlines a number of principles that should characterise any attempt to bring human rights into the accounting and business curricula and to articulate human rights and sustainability. This paper also presents the case for incorporating human rights into business and accounting education at both tertiary and professional levels, particularly with the growing number of cases in which large multinational corporations have been complicit in human rights violations. Whilst accepting the not insignificant challenges of integrating human rights into accounting curricula, Andrew is fully supportive of the ideas expressed by McPhail, and offers further support to the initiatives outlined in his paper and the importance of designing educational interventions that do not preach but which encourage students to engage critically with the possibility that accounting and businesses may be able to help realise the universal declaration of human rights and not unwittingly support human right abuses. Everett commends and fully supports McPhail for tackling the relationship between human rights and accounting, but expresses concerns over the feasibility of doing so. Everett agrees that human rights should be in a business school's curriculum, but remains unconvinced that business schools will be receptive to the idea of a human rights-oriented business curriculum. In his Commentary he outlines the range and extent of the challenges that need to be confronted and overcome if human rights and sustainability are to become fully integrated into business and accounting curricula. However, this Commentary also incorporates a number of constructive suggestions as to how the objectives expressed in McPhail are to be realised. These include business curricula starting from a position in which human actors are seen as moral actors having moral obligations to others and existing in a world where responsibilities are as important as rights. In this curriculum the pedagogy should promote questions about the nature and legitimate use of power and authority, and explicitly consider accounting for human rights and sustainability disclosures as conduits of power, not the communication of

business and management discipline more generally.[2] The academic literature that has emerged from this exercise is itself voluminous. Within this (particularly accounting education) literature there are a number of seams that provide elements of the departure point for the present paper. These elements might be typified as: student resistance to innovation; the ethically stultifying impact of accounting education; and the reluctance, even refusal, of students (and often times teachers) to consider anything that cannot be reduced to economic calculus (Gray, Bebbington and McPhail, 1994, 2001; McPhail, 1999; Collison et al., 2000; Gray and Collison, 2002; Mayper et al., 2005; Ferguson et al., 2011). All of these concerns are made explicitly manifest when one is seeking to integrate social and/or environmental matters into the classroom orthodoxy (Collison et al., 2000; Collison, Ferguson and Stevenson, 2007), and become crucial when the demands of sustainability are considered (Lozano, 2006; Sipos, Battisti and Grimm, 2008).

There are a number of excellent reviews of accounting education that formally address the tensions between the conventions of accounting education and the challenges of a more social and environmental orientation (see, for example, Thomson and Bebbington, 2004; Collison, Ferguson and Stevenson, 2007). Indeed, social and environmental accounting itself has a particularly striking tradition in exploring these matters (see, for example, Mathews, 1995, 2001; Lockhart and Mathews, 2000). The social and environmental accounting education literature has demonstrated how, through innovation, persistence and engagement, the subject has developed as a field; from one with almost no presence in the accounting academy to a tolerated, even a welcome, guest within many schools (see, for example, Lewis, Humphrey and Owen, 1992; Owen, Humphrey and Lewis, 1994; Stevenson, 2002; Gordon, 2007; Thomson, 2007; and, in a wider context, Lozano, 2006).

In the light of this extensive academic accounting literature, and especially in the light of the continuing interest shown by social and environmental accounting academics in matters of education, the relative dearth of papers specifically addressing sustainability and accounting education was unexpected. Whilst there *is* an important literature that addresses accounting and sustainability education, only a small proportion of this relatively small band of papers appears to directly address the deep challenges that sustainability presents, both in the classroom and more broadly.[3] It is beyond the scope and competence of this paper to fully address why this might be, but this certainly looks like an issue on which future research might well prove fruitful (a matter considered briefly in the conclusions to the paper).

Before entering the body of the paper, there is, however, one crucial issue which will influence a lot of what follows. That is the issue of 'conflict', both political and psychological. Psychological conflict should arguably be an essential of mainstream accounting, finance and management education (McPhail, 2004; Thomson and Bebbington, 2004). Accounting educators, it would seem, have considerable potential to exploit the opportunities for shock, cognitive dissonance and other intellectually disruptive techniques (Lucas, 2008; Gorski, 2009). And this is precisely what a critical pedagogy informed, to some degree at least, by the insights of critical accounting or critical management studies might embrace. But it is precisely this which is so essential to but so starkly absent from (all but a small minority of) the sustainability and accounting/finance/management education literature. The relationships between environmental sustainability, social justice, accounting and corporations are themselves essentially issues of conflict (Gladwin, Newburry and Reiskin, 1997) and, it seems to follow, failure to address that conflict leaves us unable to address the issues themselves. To address sustainability, accountability, accounting and corporations involves at least a minimum recognition that only through an analysis of hegemonic claims and assumptions can we gain any traction on the matter.

Consider the following. If, for the sake of argument, we were to assume that corporate social responsibility (CSR) and sustainability were equivalent ideas and that both were not only compatible with the organisation's conventional pursuit of (accounting) profit,[4] but essential to it, then worrying about whether and/or how organisations can or should be sustainable and responsible is largely a waste of time: the market will clearly resolve the matter (Orlitsky, Schmidt and Rynes, 2003; Oberndorfer, 2004). That is, if the pursuit by organisations of the highest standards of environmental and social probity were essential to the maximisation of shareholder wealth, then it would only be the less able organisations that would not be doing exactly this. Financial markets are designed (we are told) precisely to weed out such wastrels. Thus, the argument might go, economically successful organisations must essentially be contributing to greater social responsibility, greater social justice and greater environmental sustainability. So when, as the majority of the literature suggests (by whatever linguistic sleight of hand we may wish to adopt), CSR and/ or sustainability are compatible with traditional economic pursuit, then we are able to conclude that by pursuing wealth we are contributing most to society and the planet. This is clearly absurd but it is an implicit (and typically unexamined) argument, which sits beneath a considerable amount of our discussions of such matters as accounting and the public interest, accountability, social responsibility and sustainability. It is too easy to suggest – as much of business and liberal belief might like to claim – that there is no conflict between what we currently consider to be economic well-being and the state of mankind and the planet. If it were the case, then the world would be growing in wealth, justice and planetary sustainability and our conventional pursuit of economic objectives would be demonstrably delivering us a sustainable future. It clearly is not (Gray, 2006a, 2006b).

As we shall confirm shortly, any claims that planetary sustainability is in safe hands are, at best, highly contentious. Equally, conclusions must be drawn with care from the CSR literature, as these studies are highly selective in what they mean by social responsibility. More pertinently, whilst social responsibility might be defined to include social and environmental sustainability, it need not be (and frequently is not). CSR is an essentially moral or instrumentalist concern (depending upon how one defines it), whilst sustainability refers to planetary data, species extinction and social and environmental inequality. So being responsible need not mean being sustainable, and vice versa. Their conflation is either lazy or (at best) mischievous.

So if it is not necessarily the case that economic pursuit, responsibility and sustainability are uncontrovertibly consonant, if it is the case (perhaps contentiously) that social responsibility is a desirable activity, if we accept (less contentiously) that sustainability is a desirable goal, and if we recognise the central implication of accounting in organisations' economic pursuits, then there is potential conflict (and a potentially profound conflict) between everything we conventionally teach in accounting and business and what a deep responsibility and a pursuit of sustainability require of us. To fail to confront that conflict is arguably an abandonment of a key duty we owe to our students, our professional values and society.

Maybe it is the case that, as accountants and as accounting academics, we are little equipped to teach conflict or to encourage and support students in its pursuit. Furthermore, our institutions themselves have many ways of subtly encouraging each of us to consider challenging the status quo as somehow improper. As Mayper et al. (2005) contend, our universities are no longer capable of the function for which they were developed. They go on to suggest that the reason why society gives universities so many privileges is that:

> corporatism [becomes] so dominant [...] that economic values permeate all other societal institutions, resulting in a loss of independence and autonomy of other societal institutions (Mayper *et al.*, 2005, p. 34; see also Thielemann, 2000)[5]

Whatever the reason, the departure point for the paper is an anxiety concerning the relative absence from the accounting education literature of the deeply challenging conflicts that sustainability essentially raises for most mainstream assumptions about accounting, business, markets and society. The objectives of the paper are strictly polemic and modest: simply to raise and expose the probable conflicts that sit unexamined within much accounting education regarding the exigencies of sustainability and to offer (and reflect upon) one example of an attempt to address this.

The paper is therefore organised as follows.

- Section 2 briefly examines what is meant by sustainability.
- Section 3 then explores whether we can find any plausible culprits for our condition of un-sustainability.
- Section 4 then moves on to look at how sustainability is represented, both within and without education, and within and without accounting and business and management.
- Section 5 introduces a taught module as one way of addressing these concerns. It has a personal emphasis and explores teaching experiences and how I think I begin to confront the students and, indeed, to get the elephant into the classroom.
- Section 6 concludes the paper with a reflection and discussion.

2. What is Sustainability?

Despite the apparent ubiquity of sustainability, it does not appear to be widely understood, nor its complexities fully appreciated (Gladwin, Kennelly and Krause, 1995a; Gladwin, Krause and Kennelly, 1995b; Bebbington and Thomson, 1996; Gladwin, Newburry and Reiskin, 1997; Gray and Bebbington, 2000; Kelly and Alam, 2009; Sky, 2012). 'Sustainability' is also an elusive and indeterminate concept.[6] It can be defined (explicitly or by implication) in a wide variety of ways, only some of which are caught by the notion of weak versus strong sustainability, summarised in Box 1 (Turner, 1993; Bebbington and Thomson, 1996). For some it is equated (as we have seen) with CSR, for some it is about eco-efficiency, for others it is transmuted into the sustainability of the business, but for many it is a notion entirely incompatible with modernity, capitalism and growth as we currently understand it (Milne, Kearins and Walton, 2006; Milne, Tregidda and Walton, 2009). It is certainly a floating, and may even be an empty, signifier (Brown and Fraser, 2006; Spence, 2007). Thus, trying to settle the epistemological status of sustainability is, in itself, a daunting task (Gray, 2010). However, if only for the purposes of this paper (and indeed within the terms of the module discussed later), there is a strong case for allowing a strong realist tinge to enter the discussion.[7] That is, there is a considerable range of empirical conditions that a progress towards sustainability needs to satisfy (to do with, for example, such matters as species extinction and social inequity), and an examination of the conflict between these empirical data and business and organisational assumptions becomes a key mechanism for 'pulling one up short' (Lucas, 2008; see also Box 2).

Box 1. Strong versus weak sustainability (adapted from Bebbington and Thomson, 1996).

EXPLORING THE NATURE OF SUSTAINABILITY		
Element	**Strong sustainability**	**Weak sustainability**
Motivation?	Re-examine relationship of and between humans and natural environment	Prevent environmental catastrophe that could threaten humanity
Nature-human relationship?	Intertwined, harmony sought	Environment is a resource, human need to master environment
What should be sustained?	All species	Some or all of humanity
Gap between sustainability and present?	Enormous, adjustment almost unimaginable: possibly 150–200 years	Relatively small: adjust in 30–50 years
Extent of change?	Fundamental, structural	Incremental adjustment
Nature of change?	(Hopefully) Participatory, transparent + democratic – not technical	Technological and (preferably) market-based
ECO-justice	Intra-generational equity essential	Focus on environment: equity is a separate matter
What sort of sustainability?	Redefine/abandon economic growth, change organisation and development	Maintain western ways of life: economic growth essential

The conventional (and probably most useful) starting point from which to explore sustainability is that of the Brundtland Report:

> Sustainable development is development that meets the needs of the present without compromising the ability of future generations to meet their own needs [...] Development involves a progressive transformation of economy and society [...] But physical sustainability cannot be secured unless development policies pay attention to such considerations as changes in access to resources and in the distribution of costs and benefits. Even the narrow notion of physical sustainability implies a concern for social equity between generations, a concern that must logically be extended to equity within each generation. (WCED, 1987, p. 43)[8]

Despite (or even because of) the generality of this definition, it has proved exceptionally helpful in articulating this crisis that humanity faces (anthropocentricity acknowledged for the time being). Typically, Brundtland-based understandings of sustainability lead us to explore both the physical state of the planet (nature, ecosystems stability, resources, life) and the social equity concerns over relative access to planetary and natural resources.

Box 2. A suggestion of social inequality.

> *If we could shrink the world to a village of 100 people, pro-rata there would be 57 Asians, 21 Europeans, 14 from the Western hemisphere, north and south, and eight Africans. Eighty would live in sub-standard housing, 70 would be unable to read, 50 would suffer malnutrition. Six would possess 59% of the world's wealth and all of them would be from the USA. Only one would own a computer.*

To what extent the Brundtland definition would encourage us to go yet further and talk (or not talk) about other more fundamental and challenging issues (most notably the destruction of culture and spirituality and/or the essential primacy of economic development) is a moot point and, although crucial to full understandings of sustainability, probably should not detain us here (see, for example, Zimmerman, 1994; Gladwin, Kennelly and Krause, 1995a; Gladwin, Krause and Kennelly, 1995b; Gladwin, Newburry and Reiskin, 1997; Dresner, 2002).

The physical data concerning the planet are almost unequivocally bad, in the sense that they show declines of life, capacities and systems upon which humanity and other life rely. It is not just climate change and certainly not just 'carbon'; it is levels of consumption and waste, peak oil, overshoot, footprints, species extinction, water shortage and so on. Wherever one derives the data and however one seeks to interpret the data, it seems very clear that humanity is (to use an accounting analogy) treating planetary capital as income. The data tells us that Western lifestyles cannot be maintained for very real physical reasons and if India and China aspire to European lifestyles, humanity will require approximately three planets. Even under very optimistic assumptions, humanity's ways of organising do not appear to be sustainable or likely to become so (for much more detail see, for example, Meadows *et al.*, 1972; Meadows, Randers and Meadows, 2004; United Nations Environment Programme (UNEP), 2002; WWF, 2004, 2008; Millennium Ecosystem Assessment, 2005).[9]

The global data about human society offer a slightly more equivocal picture (UNDP, 2010), in that longevity and education have never been higher but inequality, for example, continues to increase. Alarming levels of starvation and drought continue to blight whole swathes of the world. Whether this is socially sustainable is difficult to judge. Inevitably, it seems, one's judgement on that data is likely to influenced by a combination of one's moral stance on the suffering of others and how fortunate one actually is in terms of one's privilege and insulation from disaster and suffering. Whilst the West is no utopia,[10] the majority[11] (although only a majority) do not lack for the basic essentials of existence. We might be ever mindful that the Millennium Development Goals show us that 1.4 billion people still live on less than $1.25 per day.[12]

The inference to be drawn from this is that current means of organisation are, almost entirely, un-sustainable. There is (almost) no counter argument to the contention that physical environmental sustainability is profoundly threatened and, to the extent that any sort of social sustainability is itself dependent upon environmental sustainability (as Brundtland argues above), the predominance of evidence would suggest that social sustainability is unfulfilled also. The final step in the reasoning is to conclude that humanity is moving *away* from sustainability – we are becoming more un-sustainable – and that all the apparent attempts of recent years may have slowed the rate of acceleration away from sustainability; they have not had any discernible impact on moves towards sustainability (York, Rosa and Dietz, 2003).

> Human activity is putting such strain on the natural functions of Earth that the ability of the planet's ecosystems to sustain future generations can no longer be taken for granted. (Millennium Eco-Assessment, 2005, p. 2)

Why this situation may obtain and how it is responded to are the subject of the next two sections.

3. Whose Fault is it? How is Sustainability Represented?

The causes of un-sustainability are, inevitably, elusive. This is such a complex situation that unequivocally identifying cause and effect is fraught. Some of the more widely shared views are that un-sustainability is a result of: governments; bureaucracy; greed; consumption; capitalism; poverty; people; religion; men; imperfections in the market; accounting; modernity; financial markets; and so on (see Zimmerman, 1994; Dresner, 2002; Kovel, 2002; Porritt, 2005 for a selection of these).That all are implicated to various degrees seems largely incontrovertible, but it is unlikely that one could unequivo-cally identify the lead culprit, and pedagogically it may well be inadvisable to do so (Gray, 2010).

Consequently it can often be helpful – especially pedagogically – to explicitly avoid focusing on any single culprit and to encourage students to explicitly recognise that un-sustainability is probably caused by some combination of civil society, the market and the state; that all of us are implicated in the situation in a variety of roles. Furthermore, it also possible (and helpful) to suggest that the more wealthy, powerful and privileged that we are, the more likely it is that we have: helped to cause the problem; and have a moral responsibility (and agency) to do something about it (Gray, Dillard and Spence, 2009). Such a position is plausible and reasonable; avoids easy victimisation; places both agency and structure in the frame; and it has the additional advantage pedagogically of making it more difficult for students (and staff) to depersonalise the issues and to try to hide behind accusations against the 'other'.

In an attempt to understand at least environmental sustainability rather better and to avoid simple accusations of fault, Erlich and Erlich (1978) proposed the heuristic:

$$I = P \times A \times T,$$

where I = impact, P = population, A = affluence and T = technology.

The notion is simple enough. Environmental impact is some combination of the number of people (P), what they consume (A), and the technology (T) that produces that consump-tion. (The technology is recognised as being both the source of the many efficiencies that industry generates (Porritt, 2005) and the source of many of the negative interactions and potentials for pollution, waste and damage.) The suggestion is only a heuristic, but one that has stood the test of time and that offers a plausible way of addressing the issues at stake.

The first issue is clearly that of population. Population is a key variable, and a matter over which we have some personal impact. It is not, as far as I can see, something upon which an accounting, finance or management scholar has a great deal of professional expertise to offer. As an informed and analytical commentator, it may be that questions of responsibility, family size, perinatal mortality and suchlike matters deserve our atten-tion and, without question, they will arise very properly in class situations. It remains unclear whether or not it is apposite to formally address such matters within the limited confines of a semi-structured course on which there is no shortage of challenging material.

So, the focus moves to affluence and technology. It hardly seems contentious to agree with business representatives, liberal thinkers and Western governments that what we nor-mally consider to be affluence (however misguided we might be) has grown massively over the last 50 years and owes much of its growth to modernity and capitalism, and, of course, to the engines of modernity and capitalism: the corporations. Equally, there is little question that a significant element in the development of technology – both benign in its pursuit of efficiency and less so its development of new and more systemic impacts – also owes its growth to the same elements.

So placing corporations at the heart of the sustainability debate seems entirely apposite: nothing is suggesting that corporations are the sole or even the main cause of un-sustainability, but they are certainly deeply and intrinsically implicated. To this extent, many radical commentators have little difficulty in agreeing with business commentators.

It is the next step(s) in the argument where difference emerges. That is, to what extent should we follow through this argument of Erlich's and infer that corporations (and modernity and capitalism) are profoundly contributing to un-sustainability. If we do this, then we can begin to look critically at how they might possibly begin to offer something to the attempts to move away from un-sustainability. However, this is precisely what business does *not* do, and here begins a major source of conflict (Gray, 2006a, 2006b, 2010; Milne, Kearins and Walton, 2006; Tregidga and Milne, 2006; Milne, Tregidga and Walton, 2009).[13]

There is much to be said on this issue (see, for example, Kovel, 2002; York, Rosa and Dietz, 2003; Henriques and Richardson, 2004), but for our purposes here it is sufficient to briefly outline two particular conflicts: how business represents itself regarding sustainability; and the essential question of whether the changes necessary to deliver sustainability are marginal or radically structural in nature (see Box 1 in this respect).

Business and business representative groups clearly expend a not insignificant amount of time, effort and, in all probability, resources to represent themselves as being 'responsible' and, increasingly, as 'sustainable'. Examples include the World Business Council for Sustainable Development (Mayhew, 1997; WBCSD, 2002, 2011; Oberndorfer, 2004); The International Chamber of Commerce (ICC, 1991); GRI (2006); BASE (Flyer for the Business and Sustainable Environment Conference, UK March 2010); even the UK's Prince of Wales 'Accounting for Sustainability Group'[14]; and, most obviously, the Dow Jones Sustainability Index. However, the representation is much more direct when practiced by the companies themselves. Two examples may suffice for now:

> The sustainability of companies, industries and the entire global financial system was tested in 2008. Halliburton weathered the turmoil by focusing on offering competitive, safe and superior-quality products and services, and on pursuing our sustainable development vision. (Halliburton, *Corporate Sustainability Report*, 2008, which, incidentally mentions sustaining or sustainable 49 times but never defines it/links it to the planet or justice)

> [Sustainability is . . .] the capacity to endure as a group, by renewing assets, creating and delivering better products and service that meet the evolving needs of society, delivering returns to our shareholders, attracting successive generations of employees, contributing to a flourishing environment and retaining the trust and support of our customers and the communities in which we operate. (*Making the Right Choices*, BP Sustainability Report, 2004)

The representations are widespread and there is a growing literature that challenges this representation (see, for example, Laine, 2005, 2010; Moneva, Archel and Correa, 2006; Milne and Gray, 2007; Milne, Ball and Gray, 2008). The conclusion that seems apposite here is to recognise that a significant proportion of business and many business organisations are exerting considerable effort to suggest one view of the world. Not only is this view of the world challenged but there is no evidence (of which I am aware) that supports this representation. This has very important implications indeed. So, for example, it seems highly likely that if business is successful in representing itself as no part of the problem and a major potential solution, then the organs of civil society and the state are much less likely to focus a critical attention upon business. Such critical attention would lead to questioning of corporations, ownership, growth, consumption, accounting, wealth and so on. The implications for discourse, and for the classroom, are probably critical. I examine some of these in the next section.

The second, and arguably more nuanced, issue at this stage concerns the central question of whether it is possible to achieve something recognisably sustainable through (predominantly) linear development based upon marginalist adaptations around eco-efficiencies and social responsibility. Alternatively, is it more or less likely that the notion of sustainability is a challenging structural notion that goes to the very heart of everything that we tend to assume about business and modernity? The latter perspective suggests that the very basis of modern accounting, the essential principles of modern international finance, the normal attachments of business to (versions of) maximising shareholder wealth, and ever increasing levels of consumption must be drastically re-assessed, if not eschewed altogether. This is what Bebbington and Thomson (1996) reference when they talk of 'weak' and 'strong' sustainability (Turner, 1993), and it is the fissure line along which sits so much of the business and sustainability debate (see, for example, Gladwin, Kennelly and Krause, 1995a; Gladwin, Krause and Kennelly, 1995b; Gladwin, Newburry and Reiskin, 1997; Gray and Bebbington, 2000; Bebbington and Gray, 2001; Jackson, 2009; Barter and Bebbington, 2010).

Such a fundamental disagreement is major and potentially life-threatening. The marginalist or weak sustainability view holds that current improvements in (such things as) taxation, technological efficiencies and improved market mechanisms, coupled with voluntary initiatives such as the Millennium Development Goals, will be sufficient to redirect global systems of organisation, consumption and finance such that a more sustainable way of doing things might emerge. The argument tends to be bolstered by the considerable and frequently stunningly impressive examples of initiative, eco-efficiencies, technological change and such like (see, for example, Porritt, 2005). The radical, structural or strong sustainability view argues that there is no evidence whatsoever to support this optimism and that, despite the immense developments in efficiencies, all that has happened is that acceleration away from sustainability has slowed down a little. Generally, the evidence seems to point to the attempts at eco-modernisation as having failed (York, Rosa and Dietz, 2003), and that drastic reductions in material consumption and waste and major redistributions of wealth are currently the only empirical bases for any potential approach to sustainability. One commentator, Bergström (1993), suggests that we need to do nothing less than to:

> [...] consider that the environment goes to the very root of what it is to be human, that the very scale and ethical accoutrements of the environmental crisis place in question all the elements of modernity. Under a structural perspective, no element of current orthodoxy – be it economic growth, distributions of wealth, the institutions of civil society, the organization of work or our concepts of consumption, production, social structure or whatever – can be taken for granted.

However uncomfortable it might be, the lack of evidence to support the marginalist view, plus the 30 years or so in which it has been unsuccessfully pursued, places the burden of proof, arguably, firmly on the marginalists (Gray, 2006a, 2006b; Milne, Kearins and Walton, 2006; Milne, Ball and Gray, 2008). Indeed, the *a priori* case seems to be that pursuit of (conventional) profit, efficiency, growth, choice, consumption and so forth is substantially and fundamentally incompatible with the principles of sustainability and *its* pursuit. More likely still, conventional accounting, finance, business strategy and capitalism are, in all probability, driving *un-sustainability* (Gray, 1990).

Upon reflection, this should not really surprise us; after all, the purpose of capitalism and the accounting system within it is (to misquote Schumpeter) a form of constant – if sometimes creative – destruction:

> [...] 93% of materials that we buy and "consume" never end up in saleable products at all. Moreover 80% of products are discarded after a single use [... and] 99% of the original material used in the production of, or contained within, the goods made in the US become waste within 6 weeks of sale. (Weizsäcker, Lovins and Lovins, 1997, p. 4)

This is not the place to fully examine the complexities of these contentions, but, optimism apart, there is a truly substantive body of argument and evidence that, whether or not one finds it completely convincing, is substantive enough to deserve careful consideration in any reasonable debate (see also Thielemann, 2000; York, Rosa and Dietz, 2003). As educationalists, what may well bother us most is that the arguments are rarely permitted into the debate and, by most pedagogic values, this is unacceptable. It is this that I turn to now.

4. Presentation in Pedagogic (and Wider Business and Management) Literature

On the face of it, there is no shortage of recognition of the panoply of issues that sustainability and/or the natural environment raise for both educators and business (see, for example, Huckle and Sterling, 1996; Gray-Donald and Selby, 2008; Jones, Selby and Sterling, 2010),[15] and there is certainly no shortage of publications that claim to address the business and sustainability issues themselves (see, for example, Dunphy, Griffiths and Benn, 2003; Thorpe and Prakash-Mani, 2003; Hitchcock and Willard, 2006; Schaltegger and Wagner, 2006; Blackburn, 2007; Epstein, 2008; Tilbury, 2011; Jain, 2011; even the Global Reporting Initiative, GRI, 2006). There are a number of issues that are striking about publications such as these. First, very little of this literature, it seems, carefully examines how (and indeed whether) the notion of global sustainability can be applied to corporations (the most obvious concern is that sustainability is a global, regional or ecosystems concept that translates only with difficulty to a construct such as 'the organisation'). Secondly, this growing and influential body of literature appears able to address 'sustainability' without ever checking whether it is, indeed, addressing anything to do with sustainability as we understand it through Brundtland. This matters, because if we believe the problem that is to be solved is sustainability, then we want solutions to address sustainability, not some anodyne analogue that bears little or no relationship with the matter at hand.[16] Equally, if an increasing proportion of managers (and those being educated in accounting and business) are quite unaware that what they are managing is something-that-is-not-quite-but-almost-entirely-unlike-sustainability (to misquote Douglas Adams), then the species (and a few others beside) is in danger of being led to oblivion by (what amounts to) a form of lotus-eating. Two illustrations of the assertions will suffice for now:

> The ICAEW is setting out to prove to business professionals around the world that there is an undeniable business case for having a sustainable development strategy. And it's working. (*Accountancy Magazine*, December 2008, p. 89)

> "business case of sustainability" [. . .] [O]r stated differently: how can the competitiveness and business success of a company be improved with voluntarily created outstanding environmental and social performance? (Schaltegger and Wagner, 2006, p. 1)

Such assertive texts are predominantly, if explicitly, aimed at a business market, but their relevance here is that not only might we anticipate leakage between business and business-education domains, but a number of the texts are also used as student textbooks; and that may well bother us even more as we know the influence of the textbook (see, for example, Ferguson *et al.*, 2011).

When we turn to look at the business and education literature itself, a number of things seem to stand out.[17] First, there is a relatively substantive literature that appears to address business education and sustainability. Stimulated in part by the growing influence of the United Nations Principles of Responsible Management Education and fostered by journals such as *Academy of Management Learning and Education*, the *Journal of Management*

Education and the *International Journal of Sustainability in Higher Education* (amongst others), there is a burgeoning exploration of how sustainability might affect and be embedded in business and management education. The literature is wider than this though and, for example, a special issue of the *Journal of Corporate Citizenship* in February 2011 focused on 'Designing Management Education' and included a piece by Whiting, de Pillis and Hatch (2011), which explicitly recognised sustainability. Other papers have appeared in such diverse journals as *Business Strategy and the Environment* and even the *Journal of Cleaner Production*.[18]

Given the diversity and dispersion of the apposite literature, it might be advisable to hold any claims that this literature review is complete or thorough. However, insofar as the review has successfully identified a representative proportion of the key literature for this paper, a number of points are quite arresting. Most strikingly, the mainstream journals show very little – if any – substantive engagement with sustainability and the issues it brings. It is always as well to remember that substantive engagement with sustainable development has yet to reach the mainstream.[19] Equally, with a few notable and admirable exceptions, it would appear that the papers in the field seem to adopt either a strictly marginalist approach to sustainability (of the 'how can sustainability help a manager' sort of thing: Thomson and Bebbington, 2004), or a more procedural focus on educational methods for introducing the words of sustainability into the classroom (Springett, 2005). Illustrations of these approaches might include Stubbs and Cocklin's (2008) intention to 'help MBA students [. . .] reconcile the different sustainability perspectives', or the more widespread (but empirically more challenging) optimism and ensuing absence of any apparent acceptance of actual or potential conflict, such as Rowe and Wehrmeyer (2010), Rusinko and Sama (2009), and Stead and Stead (2010). Perhaps this should not surprise us, as management (and accounting) education largely retains a predominantly managerialist orientation and management education was notoriously slow to embrace CSR and ethics in education (Swanson, 2005). However, these observations become frustrating when one tries to engage with this literature, because even pieces by those with impeccable credentials in the field (see especially Starik *et al.*, 2010; Stead and Stead, 2010) would seem unable to confront the challenges and conflicts that the exigencies of sustainability really present. This review was unable to unearth much that confronted the uncomfortable, the conflictual, the challenging. Very little confronted fundamental matters such as the role and existence of markets, consumption, organisations or growth. It all seemed a bit too safe and comfortable.

But any notion of sustainability – especially one in education – should really (as Martin, 2011 suggests) keep you awake at night. Martin goes on to suggest that maybe:

> the reason why sustainability only keeps a few people awake at night is that it is complex and confusing and hence difficult to decide what to do.

Martin's claims are persuasive and offer a telling heuristic with which to try and assess, more exactly, whether or not the accounting literature looked as though it might be keeping students awake. One might approach such a question with initial optimism, as there does seem to be a much more substantial literature on accounting and sustainability than there is on management and sustainability, especially given the relative sizes of the communities (although see Springett, 2005 for a challenging illustration of how management students are kept awake at night).

I confess to being surprised by how little literature there seemed to be that directly addressed accounting education and sustainability. Given the real importance of accounting education within the accounting academy, the long history of social and environmental accounting academics active in education research, and the prominence of sustainability in areas of the wider accounting literature, one might have reasonably anticipated a substantial body of work in the field. Allowing for oversights within this literature review, even the appropriate literature of substance seemed to contain little reference to other work in our discipline (see Chulian, 2011 for confirmation of this point). Similar to the experience with the management literature, there were examples of procedural[20] explorations (see, for example, Cowton, 2004; Coulson and Thomson, 2006; Hazelton and Haigh, 2010; Chulian, 2011), but, in contrast with the management literature, there appears to be a much greater emphasis on reflection (see, for example, Bebbington, 2007; Gray et al., 2001; Gray and Collison, 2002; Thomson and Bebbington, 2004, 2005; Collison, Ferguson and Stevenson, 2007; Kelly and Alam, 2009). What these reflections did not do, as far as I could see (and I qualify this assertion shortly), was help an educator really bring the cold wind of sustainability into the classroom and confront the data and the potential conflicts and challenges that sustainability raises.

It is at this point that one might begin to explicitly confront one's own pedagogical allegiances (Thomson and Bebbington, 2004; Lucas, 2008). To do so is disturbing in that most accounting academics are not educational theorists and are not trained in educational reflection. Our pedagogic experiences and expertise, whilst informed by the literature, are likely to have a strong experiential and deductive element to them. Such is the case in what follows. The exploration of any pedagogic allegiances comes only as a result of having sought to follow instinct in education and trying to reflect upon it in order to make some sense of it (Lucas, 2002).

5. A Case Study

Mayper et al. (2005) posit that 'our current accounting educational environment should be expected to desensitize students to the ethical aspects of their profession' (p. 32), and there is certainly a variety of evidence that is consistent with this contention (McPhail, 1999; Collison et al., 2000; Ferguson et al., 2011). However, there are also many examples of teaching practice that suggest that this state of affairs need not necessarily obtain (Coulson and Thomson, 2006). What there is not – as far as I can see – is evidence of examples of an educational engagement that formally addresses the conflicting views and (lack of) evidence around sustainability and explores what this means – if anything – for management, organisations and business and accounting. The following is a reflection on one of the modules that I teach at the University of St Andrews. It hardly classes as formal or persuasive evidence per se, but it offers an example of one approach to seeking to prevent students from sleeping at night.

Kelly and Alam (2009), quoting approvingly from the New Zealand Parliamentary Commission for the Environment, suggest that:

> Ultimately, education for sustainability requires people to critically think about and reflect on their own values and the values embedded in the institutions that surround them. (PCE, 2004, quoted in Kelly and Alam, 2009, p. 32)

Such sentiments are widely expressed in explorations of the demands of sustainability education (see, for example, UNESCO, 2011). What is less obvious is what form that 'critical thinking' should take.

Thomson and Bebbington (2004) interestingly juxtapose Ivan Illich and Paulo Freire as theorists of transformative education and famously settle on the dialogic tradition of Freire as their guiding principle (Thomson and Bebbington, 2004, 2005; Coulson and Thomson, 2006). Despite attempts to really engage with this idea (Gray, 2010), I confess to finding more sympathy with Illich and his tradition. As Kahn and Kellner (2007) persuasively argue, whilst the dichotomy may be more imagined than real, Illich's 'oppositional concepts of education' (p. 442) help us exploit cognitive dissonance in the educational process. It is my contention that, if substantive analysis, seriously reflective thinking and confrontation of conflict are to take place, they may be best achieved through cognitive dissonance. Such a commitment, which might be termed the *phenomenology of disruption*,[21] is based upon the hypothesis that new views and new insights will be most easily examined when there is serious intellectual discomfort. This discomfort is achieved through the steady exposure to different groups of evidence and reasoning and the juxtaposition of these. In the conventional mechanism of the debate or the essay, the student is then required to confront the arguments and evidence that does not fit with (what they believe to be) their worldview,[22] or where they are holding two cognitions simultaneously.[23] The notion is not new (see, for example, Gorski, 2009) and the approach is referred to in critical ethnomethodology as 'breaching':

> Breaching must be radical because people will naturally assimilate strange situations into familiar ones, and in order to cause disruption, one must create a radical enough breach that it cannot be normally constructed. ((Hippen, Yates and Mason, n.d.)

And whilst there is a recognition of this need for insistent questioning and the confronting of incompatible cognitions (Stubbs and Cocklin, 2008; Arbuthnott, 2009; Adams *et al.*, 2011), the mechanisms through which it might be achieved and then followed through seemed elusive. For this reason the module reported upon below works very hard to encourage and engage dialogue throughout the teaching process. But much more important than that, I suspect, is the choice and examination of the subject matter of the course; the nature of the dialogue which is 'allowed'; the importance of evidence and reasoning and an almost brutal indifference (I'll qualify this later) to what the students 'feel' (Thomson and Bebbington, 2004; Lucas, 2008). I explicitly want students who will not sleep at night. The module I now outline (and my reasons for outlining it) is not simply to offer a counter to the claims of business concerning responsibility and sustainability, although that is important. As we will see, it is more that such claims might be engaged with analytically, and that these and other future claims might then be treated in a more hopeful and intelligent manner.

The module is a first-semester undergraduate honours option module entitled *Corporate Social Responsibility, Accountability and Reporting*. The students are a mix of third- and fourth-year honours students in management (single and joint degrees), plus students from the sustainable development undergraduate degree. In addition, there are always a few visitors, tourists, visiting faculty and doctoral students who attend. The module is *not* strictly an accounting module; the St Andrews degree in management is *not* accredited and has very little accounting within it. An initial advantage I have is that St Andrews students are great students to teach: on the whole very bright, enthusiastic and engaged and very, very responsive to challenge. That the students are not accounting majors has advantages and disadvantages. On the one hand, a lack of accounting knowledge is something of a problem in that their focus tends not to be on information and accountability and their base knowledge of markets and capital is slim. On the other hand, the lack of accreditation and the associated self-disciplining (Gray *et al.*, 2001) and discipline definition that so pervades accounting (Hopwood, 2007) is not a issue. Further, in a way that I still find strange, I have almost complete freedom over what I teach and how I teach it. As we have discovered in other contexts, the level of self-disciplining to which accounting academics subject themselves as teachers is only really matched by that exhibited by the students (Gray *et al.*, 2001).

Box 3. Coursework options.

Coursework Choice 1: Compile a detailed review and critique of: Bakan, J. (2004) *The Corporation: The Pathological Pursuit of Profit and Power* (London: Constable and Robinson). Ensure that the review articulates with the wider relevant literature.

Coursework Choice 2: Produce a Shadow and/or Silent Account of the company of your choice. Details can be found on the CSEAR website under 'Approaches to Practice'.

Coursework Choice 3: Advise the Dow Chemical Company what they should do about Bhopal.

Coursework Choice 4: Produce a detailed, *systematic* and ***justified*** critique of one organisation's approach to social, environmental and sustainability reporting.

Coursework Choice 5: Provide an analytical response relating to *either* accountability or responsibility to the Executive Summary of the scenarios *either* 'Tribal Trading' *or* 'Good Intentions'.

The module's formal contact comprises 10 weekly two-hour interactive lectures plus weekly small group interactive tutorials; the latter are probably the most important part of the course. The module is examined by an unseen examination (60%) and two pieces of coursework for 20% each. The second piece of coursework is an individual analytical and critical essay chosen from a wide range of questions. The first piece is a group project in which each group chooses one of five options (see Box 3).

The course is explicitly designed to encourage (almost require, actually) the student to find his/her own voice and come to an informed view – however tentative – about the relationship that he/she holds personally with large corporations, financial markets, CSR and sustainability. The central question that the course seeks to answer is: 'To what extent, if at all, can (especially quoted) corporations be profitable and responsible/sustainable?' It is very demanding. The opening session explains this, promises them support throughout the module and tells them that if they cannot manage this more complex discussion, there are a series of 'topics' at the end, which, in addition to the coursework topics, provide a more conventional basis around which they can build their understandings and articulations.[24] We discuss the terms of engagement (the classes must always exhibit respect and the only currencies must be evidence and argument) and the standards to be applied (Bloom's taxonomy of learning conveniently illustrates levels of reasoning that are also used as a marking template; the terms and standards of the course are those present in the medium + level English language academic journals). There is a lot of reading for the course.

The module then proceeds to lay out the (scary) stuff of sustainability, to explain a variety of theories as to how politics and the economy (civil society, the state and the market) work together, and this leads nicely into Friedman's dictum about social responsibility of business, how this is justified and how it might (or might not) be working. We then review the enormous literature on CSR before getting onto the series of 'topics' (see Box 4 and the selected reading in the Appendix to the paper; the module draws from Gray, Owen and Adams, 1996, and its currently-being-revised next edition).

Box 4. CSR lecture topics.

1: Overview of business, society, sustainability, accountability and responsibility;
2: Systems thinking, liberal democracy and social accounting;
3: Accountability, neo-pluralism and theories of organisational accountability
4: Social Responsibility and Sustainability
5: Profit and Responsibility: Conflict or Harmony?
6: Social, Environmental and 'Sustainability' Reporting
7: Environmental Management and 'win-win'
8: Socially Responsible Investment?
9: External Social Audits
10: The practice and theory of discharging social, environmental and sustainability accountability.
11: Practical options for the future?

Behind this, we meet weekly (or sometimes more if need be) to discuss the readings, the lectures and confusions. These tutorials *have* to involve high levels of student engagement or they are a waste of time (this is largely informed by a determination to avoid 'banking', but it is also based upon a belief that only if the students begin to speak the conflicts will 'breaching' occur).Tutorials are alternated: one prescribed and student-active tutorial[25] followed by one discursive, 'what are your issues?' type of tutorial. Unsupported assertion and lack of reading are not tolerated; *any* form of questioning is supported fully. Students are constantly challenged and made to feel uncomfortable, to expose and examine their cognitive dissonances, *but* there is no explicit 'party-line', there is no simple demonisation of business, politicians, capitalism, modernity or whatever (if there *are* demons and/or angels in our discourse, they are so defined by the students who must then examine, deconstruct and justify the categorisation). I consider this to be a *really* important part of the learning contract and the only thing I seek to demonise is patent dishonesty, contradiction, selected use of evidence and/or lazy reasoning. The problems are too complex to lend themselves to simple and knee-jerk solutions.[26]

Equally, it seems to be essential to get the students to realise that the course is not 'anti-business' and has immense respect for (good?) organisations and managers, but that this doesn't prevent corporations from doing 'bad things' or being selective with the truth of their public utterances. So, as well as exposing cognitive dissonance, we have to, all of us, hold potentially conflicting notions simultaneously and seek to resolve them.[27] It is here, I think, that the educational progress is really made. There is no requirement at all that students conform to certain views; they simply must be able to substantiate those views and rigorously recognise why they hold them in the face of counter-evidence and counter-pressure. Axioms, beliefs and hope are all important, but only when recognised as such.

My assessment of the course's success (or otherwise) is derived from: my own experiences; the students' apparent level of engagement (especially in tutorials but also outside in the street and after graduation); the nature (not necessarily the quality) of the written work; and the dreaded course feedback forms. The course is exhausting for me: not just the challenge and concentration I face when physically with the students, but the constant monitoring of their progress and the endless emails from the students querying this, that and the other. The learning contract is obviously two-way and very demanding.

The outcomes are fabulous educationally. In the examination almost no two answers are the same: they come from a wide variety of perspectives, literatures and beliefs to offer a variety of careful arguments around the key issues. One student might focus exclusively on sustainability, another might try to understand capitalism, yet another might take morality and responsibility as their theme, whilst a fourth might be obsessed with accountability or the role of the individual (I take this diversity as the greatest achievement of the students). And the course appraisal sheets (despite the odd annoyance and hatred of the course) are a joy: 'You really made me think, you ba****d'; 'This is what I thought University was for'; 'I thought I believed in the importance of growth and the market but I don't think I do any more'; 'You're wrong of course and Friedman was right: but at least I know why now'; and so on.

And as for sustainability? The first objective is to confront the students with the data. The key thing then is to manage and engage with the shock that the data generates. (It remains a surprise to me that so few of these educated individuals are 'aware' of the problems, in the sense that even if they know about ecological footprints or species extinction, or levels of waste and/or inequality (say), they have rarely internalised it. They rarely seem to 'own' a sense of sustainability.) Once they are confronted by these data the class's first task is to refuse to permit denial of the data ('I don't believe that'; 'that's nonsense isn't it') on the primary ground that this can only lead to closed conversations.

The un-sustainability data are supported wherever necessary and then the module develops with careful and consistent follow through: *this is not a series of topics but the development of (for each student) a course as a single argument*. The point of the follow through is to carefully explore what this means for assumptions, for business and for individuals. The support is to provide both intellectual support for what they wish to explore and test, as well as support for them personally when they confront their (previously unexamined) assumptions about career, income, success and, most telling of all, their reactions in other modules. Obviously I have neither the data nor the chutzpah to claim that the module is transformative, but, for a while, a group of intelligent young people are explicitly suffering a form of cognitive dissonance, they appreciate the size of the problem we face and they see that neither despair nor denial are options. They learn to imagine that a world of controlled financial markets, reduced consumptions, honest claims by organisations and, of course, substantive and reliable accountability, when coupled with the possibilities offered by shadow accounts, social enterprise and protest, would be a great deal different from that we currently face and, possibly, might even suggest sustainability. At least for a little while, I have a few bright people who cannot sleep!

6. Discussion

This paper has taken its departure point as a key problem (potentially) facing all educators. This problem comprises two elements: how should we bring sustainability into the classroom? and, more challengingly, how can we justify teaching anything that (at a minimum) is not obviously compatible with a growing body of very disturbing (un-sustainability) data? There would seem to be no simple answer to either question and the literature is only partially helpful to us. The second of the two questions would benefit from empirical input. Whilst we know a fair bit about how and why social and environmental accounting is (or is not) taught in the UK and elsewhere (Collison, Ferguson and Stevenson, 2007), we know much less about the accounting (and business) teaching of sustainability as such. Moreover, it is notable that the Collison, Ferguson and Stevenson review did not attempt to draw any crucial distinctions between social and environmental accounting on the one hand and the challenges of sustainability on the other. The contention throughout this paper (and, indeed, throughout the module) is that it is highly probable that sustainability (and certainly strong sustainability) changes everything: our institutions, our assumptions and understandings of the world. Whilst much of the social and environmental accounting literature is motivated by a dissatisfaction with modern ways of organising and accounting, sustainability raises that concern to one that potentially embraces life and death. And herein lies a central pedagogic challenge that brings us back to the first question. If sustainability is to be understood as 'weak sustainability', then the matter can sit alongside CSR and social and environmental accounting in the pedagogic canon. If sustainability is to be understood as 'strong sustainability', then it probably cannot. How can we engage our students to recognise this difference and to honestly come to informed opinions about such an elusive issue? If all students are to be allowed to find their own route through this problem and are not to be frightened into immobility, they must be in position, it seems to me, to explore both the structural and the managerial options that sustainability appears to suggest. This is pedagogy founded on ambiguity I think.

This paper has had deliberately modest aims. In particular, it has only sought to offer one way of engaging accounting, business and management students in order that they might confront the implications of sustainability for themselves, their careers and their discipline. The module is *not* 'about' sustainability but it is about organisations, responsibility and accountability: the context for that, as with everything, I think, is sustainability. This module (and its predecessors) has sought to explicitly address responsibility and accountability in a context of sustainability. It has grown out of the years of teaching social and environmental accounting and accountability. (That teaching inevitably reflected a combination of my level of understanding at the time plus whatever form of teaching and/or engagement I judged was possible within the constraints we all face, depending on institution and students.) The genesis of this teaching was a focus on the raw materials of accounting, business and management (i.e. organisations, managers, decisions, financial markets, control, accountability and so on), and a questioning of how one might develop a deeply analytical and uncomfortably challenging module that privileges only evidence and argument, denies *any* shallow learning, but that does not leave the student lost or floundering. This module is the result and it continues to evolve.

The exercise of developing the module and writing this paper have both required a (not always comfortable) honest confronting of one's own limitations and understandings in the face of sustainability. It has been necessary to work alongside the students in order to try and establish what it really means to us personally. This, in turn, has raised questions about personal levels of understanding and insight and what this means for the life/lives we lead. It has clearly challenged me to examine as best I can what my pedagogic allegiances and intentions might be. When that has been done, then one can humbly think about how to engage the students; *in effect to give them the course you wish you had had.*

Disruption is unlikely to be enough. Indeed, it seems very likely that education itself is not going to be enough (although some of the alternatives are genuinely frightening). Whilst that may well prove to be an empirical question (and worthy of investigation in all likelihood), the driving ethic is probably to be as good a teacher as one can. I make no bones about a lack of high moral ground; I make no bones about the fact that I fly and use a car; but I also make no bones about doing what one can. Not being able to 'do' is no excuse for not understanding, in exactly the same way as understanding will not necessary lead to doing. We do what we can. And then we don't sleep at night.

Acknowledgements

I am pleased to acknowledge the early helpful suggestions from Neil Marriott, Ian Thomson and Sue Gray. Additional comments from the participants at the BAFA Special Interest Group on Accounting Education Conference, Winchester, May 2011, and especially those from Alan Sangster and Ursula Lucas are very much appreciated. The guidance and stimulation of two anonymous reviewers is gratefully acknowledged, as is the help from Ian Thomson in bringing the paper to fruition.

Notes

[1]At least the quotation is widely attributed to Burke, although a range of scholars suggest that the exact quotation cannot be found.

[2]This is an assertion, but one which is consistent with the continuing presence of journals such as *Accounting Education: an international journal*, *Issues in Accounting Education*, *Academy of Management Learning and Education*, *Journal of Management Education*. Equally, there is a rich literature of education papers in a range of more generalist journals in accounting, finance and management. The emergence of initiatives such as the UK's Higher Education Academy also speaks to this claim.

[3]I seek to support this contentious assertion later in the paper.

[4]For the sake of simplicity, we can assume here that accounting profit represents the market-based goal of the corporation, especially those for which shares are traded in financial markets. It is fully recognised that this over-simplifies the assumed motivation and goals of the organisation and that the ubiquity of the business case is a very much more complex issue. This, however, is a matter beyond the scope of the present paper.

[5]There is an interesting irony that such observation might suggest that the sort of courses I will advocate are impossible and, more specifically, that the types of courses I teach may be threatened. The irony lies in the probable explanation that, as the students to whom the course is delivered are largely privileged and well-connected, they can be allowed to engage in seditious enquiry; somebody needs to know what the real issues are.

[6]This matter includes the obvious statement that there are a potentially infinite number of ways in which a species and a planet might coexist and therefore in which sustainability might be defined. Perceptions and dominance of a Western notion of what this entails are also illuminating (Collins and Kearins, 2010).

[7]The purpose of this is to offer a challenge to evidence-free claims of powerful and competing discourses. Brutally, a lack of a drink of water for one's child or an inability to protect that child against rape are not (at least in my world) discourse categories (Gray, 2010).

[8]I acknowledge this particular derivation of the Brundtland definition from Kelly and Alam (2009, p. 30). Conventionally, sustainable development is a process through which the state of sustainability might be achieved.

[9]For a digest of related and stimulating but largely depressing nuggets of statistics and data see www.gatt. org/. The page purports to be a WTO site but in all probability it is not!

[10]It does seem clear that life satisfaction and well-being do not increase with economic measures and social cohesion declines with inequality (Jackson, 2009).

[11]Save the Children argued that 1.6 million children in the UK live in 'severe poverty' (*Guardian*, 23 February 2011, p. 16).

[12]Such data can be misleading, not just in that the amount is so small but it can disguise its susceptibility to (mainly) food price rises: something which became acute in 2010/2011 and, according to the World Bank, dragged a further 40 million into real poverty. Larry Elliott, 'World bank warns of threat of soaring food prices', *Guardian*, 16 February 2011, p. 23.

[13]There is a lovely aphorism that states that 'the root of all human mistakes, [is] people putting things right, before they have finished finding out what is wrong'. Quoted by Neal Acherson, *Observer*, 20 March 2011, p. 41.

[14]http://www.accountingforsustainability.org/home/

[15]In addition, of course, there are a range of excellent support sources, of which the stimulating and lively Higher Education Academy's Education for Sustainable Development project on www.heacademy.ac. uk/esd is well worthy of note.

[16]Examples of the analogues included the immediate sustainability of the enterprise itself and assumptions that (for example) eco-efficiency, win-win opportunities and technological investment are sufficient to deliver a sustainable future. I remain entirely unaware of any evidence to this effect and there is legion evidence that counters it.

[17]See Quinn, Gaughran and Burke (2009) for a development of this case into engineering education.

[18]For illustration, see Walck (2009); Rusinko and Sama (2009); Clark (2010); Rusinko (2010); Rowe and Wehrmeyer (2010), Wilhelm (2008); Springett (2005); Christensen *et al.* (2007); Thomas (2005); Kearins and Springett (2003); Bergeå *et al.* (2006); Starik *et al.* (2010); Shrivastava (2010) and see Rands and Starik (2009) for more detail.

[19]It is hardly scientific but nevertheless illustrative that the last two publishers' catalogues I consulted, Sage Business and Management and Oxford Business and Economics, had no reference to sustainability or sustainable development at all, and the Sage one had no reference to environmental issues either.

[20]That is exploring the steps through which an innovation was introduced and the processes that supported it and emerged from it.

[21]I am grateful to one of the anonymous referees for this term. I have been unable to trace down the origins or even the full meanings of the term but in trying to do so I have engaged with a range of challenging work that forces me to ask what I think I am trying to do with these young people. In a sense, the referee has engaged in precisely this *phenomenology of disruption*.

[22]Trivial examples are useful here. Students believe themselves to be responsible and committed to sustainable development but go shopping on a weekly basis and throw perfectly good stuff away. Students only have two feet but have *n* pairs of shoes. Somebody is 'causing' unsustainability, and it is probably not just the poor people.

[23]The most prominent being that corporations can be responsible, sustainable and profitable. There is no evidence for this unless one defines these terms in very trivial ways.

[24]These topics still do not encourage 'banking' (Thomson and Bebbington, 2004), but recognise that different students have different capacities for intellectual discomfort and cognitive dissonance. For some, making an intellectual choice is exceptionally disturbing. The students at least learn that there are implied consequences to that inability.

[25]Examples of these include: five-minute reviews of articles; presentation of the group project; bring a list of three things that annoy, excite or confuse you; and – the most successful if exhausting – dialectic very small group work.

[26]Incidentally, one interesting (and initially unexpected) theme that emerges every year in the course is that a substantial minority of students want 'solutions'. This is, of course, admirable and something to be sought, but only when we know what problem we are seeking to solve. As a consequence, more of the module is spent trying to identify the parameters of the 'problem' than is spent offering solutions. Some students are frustrated by this; I try to use that frustration.

[27]I introduce them early on to my version of John Keats' *Negative Capability*: 'I believe absolutely in X whilst accepting without reservation that not-X may be the case'. This seems to help!

References

Adams, C. A., Heijltjes, M. G., Jack, G., Marjoribanks, T. and Powell, M. (2011) The development of leaders able to respond to climate change and sustainability challenges: the role of business schools, *Sustainability Accounting, Management and Policy Journal*, 2(1), pp. 165–171.

Arbuthnott, K. D. (2009) Education for sustainable development beyond attitude change, *International Journal of Sustainability in Higher Education*, 10(2), pp. 152–163.

Barter, N. and Bebbington, J. (2010) *Pursuing Environmental Sustainability*, Research Report 116 (London: ACCA).

Bebbington, J. (2007) *Accounting for Sustainable Development Performance* (London: CIMA).

Bebbington, K. J. and Gray, R. H. (2001) An account of sustainability: failure, success and a reconception, *Critical Perspectives on Accounting*, 12(5), pp. 557–587.

Bebbington, K. J. and Thomson, I. (1996) *Business Conceptions of Sustainability and the Implications for Accountancy* (London: ACCA).

Bergeå, O., Karlsson, R., Hedlund-Åström, A., Jacobsson, P. and Luttropp, C. (2006) Education for sustainability as a transformative learning process: a pedagogical experiment in EcoDesign doctoral education, *Journal of Cleaner Production*, 14(15–16), pp. 1431–1442.

Bergström, S. (1993) Value standards in sub-sustainable development: on limits of ecological economics, *Ecological Economics*, 7(1), pp. 1–18.

Blackburn, W. R. (2007) *The Sustainability Handbook: The Complete Management Guide to Achieving Social, Economic and Environmental Responsibility* (London: Earthscan).

Brown, J. and Fraser, M. (2006) Approaches and perspectives in social and environmental accounting: an overview of the conceptual landscape, *Business Strategy and the Environment*, 15(2), pp. 103–117.

Christensen, L., Peirce, E., Hartman, L., Hoffman, W. and Carrier, J. (2007) Ethics, CSR, and sustainability education in the *Financial Times* top 50 global business schools: baseline data and future research directions, *Journal of Business Ethics*, 73(4), pp. 347–368.

Chulian, M. F. (2011) Constructing new accountants: the role of sustainability education, *Revista de Contabilidad*, 14(Special Issue), pp. 241–265.

Clark, T. S. (2010) Management education for global sustainability, *Academy of Management Learning & Education*, 9(3), pp. 552–553.

Collins, E. M. and Kearins, K. (2010) Delivering on sustainability's global and local orientation, *Academy of Management Learning and Education*, 9(3), pp. 499–506.

Collison, D. J., Gray, R. H., Owen, D. L., Sinclair, D. and Stevenson, L. (2000) Social and environmental accounting and student choice: an exploratory research note, *Accounting Forum*, 24(2), pp. 170–186.

Collison, D., Ferguson, J. and Stevenson, L. (2007) Sustainability accounting and education, in: J. Unerman, J. Bebbington and B. O'Dwyer (Eds) *Sustainability Accounting and Accountability*, pp. 327–344 (London: Routledge).

Coulson, A. and Thomson, I. (2006) Accounting and sustainability, encouraging a dialogical approach: integrating learning activities, delivery mechanisms and assessment strategies, *Accounting Education: An International Journal*, 15(3), pp. 261–273.

Cowton, C. J. (2004) Accounting education for sustainability, in: J. Blewitt and C. Cullingford (Eds.), *The Sustainability Curriculum: The Challenge for Higher Education*, pp. 157–165 (London: Earthscan).

Dresner, S. (2002) *The Principles of Sustainability* (London: Earthscan).

Dunphy, D., Griffiths, A. and Benn, S. (2003) *Organizational Change for Corporate Sustainability: A Guide for Leaders and Change Agents of the Future* (London: Routledge).

Epstein, M. J. (2008) *Making Sustainability Work: Best Practices in Managing and Measuring Corporate Social, Environmental and Economic Impacts* (Sheffield: Greenleaf).

Erlich, P. R. and Erlich, A. H. (1978) Humanity at the crossroads, *Stamford Magazine*, Spring/Summer 1978 reprinted in Daly, H. E. (Ed.) (1980) *Economy, Ecology, Ethics: Essays Toward a Steady State Economy*, pp. 38–43 (San Francisco: W.H. Freeman).

Ferguson, J., Collison, D., Power, D. and Stevenson, L. (2011) Accounting education, socialisation and the ethics of business, *Business Ethics: A European Review*, 20(1), pp. 12–29.

Gladwin, T. N., Kennelly, J. J. and Krause, T.-S. (1995a) Shifting paradigms for sustainable development: implications for management theory and research, *Academy of Management Review*, 20(4), pp. 874–907.

Gladwin, T. N., Krause, T.-S. and Kennelly, J. J. (1995b) Beyond eco-efficiency: towards socially sustainable business, *Sustainable Development*, 3, pp. 35–43.

Gladwin, T. N., Newburry, W. E. and Reiskin, E. D. (1997) Why is the Northern elite mind biased against community, the environment and a sustainable future? in: M. H. Bazerman, D. Messick, A. Tenbrunsel and K. A. Wade-Benzoni (Eds) *Environment, Ethics and Behaviour: The Psychology of Environmental Valuation and Degradation*, pp. 234–274 (San Francisco: New Lexington).

Global Reporting Initiative (GRI) (2006) 'G3 sustainability reporting guidelines', Global Reporting Initiative. Available at http://www.globalreporting.org

Gordon, I. M. (2007) The challenge for social accounting, in: R. H. Gray and J. Guthrie (Eds) *Social Accounting, Mega-Accounting and Beyond: A Festschrift in Honour of M. R. Mathews*, pp. 23–34 (St Andrews: CSEAR Publishing).

Gorski, P. C. (2009) *Cognitive Dissonance: A Critical Tool in Social Justice Teaching*, October. Available at http://www.EdChange.org

Gray, R. (2006a) Social, environmental, and sustainability reporting and organisational value creation? Whose value? Whose creation? *Accounting, Auditing and Accountability Journal*, 19(3), pp. 319–348.

Gray, R. (2006b) Does sustainability reporting improve corporate behaviour? Wrong question? Right time? *Accounting and Business Research (International Policy Forum)*, 36, pp. 65–88.

Gray, R. (2010) Is accounting for sustainability actually accounting for sustainability … and how would we know? An exploration of narratives of organisations and the planet, *Accounting, Organizations and Society*, 35(1), pp. 47–62.

Gray, R. H. (1990) *The Greening of Accountancy: The Profession after Pearce* (London: ACCA).

Gray, R. H. and Bebbington, K. J. (2000) Environmental accounting, managerialism and sustainability: is the planet safe in the hands of business and accounting? *Advances in Environmental Accounting and Management*, 1, pp. 1–44.

Gray, R. H., Bebbington, K. J. and McPhail, K. (1994) Teaching ethics and the ethics of accounting teaching: educating for immorality and a case for social and environmental accounting education, *Accounting Education: An International Journal*, 3(1), pp. 51–75.

Gray, R. H. and Collison, D. J. (2002) Can't see the wood for the trees, can't see the trees for the numbers? Accounting education, sustainability and the public interest, *Critical Perspectives on Accounting*, 13(5/6), pp. 797–836.

Gray, R. H. and Collison, D. J. with French, J., McPhail, K., and Stevenson, L. (2001) *The Professional Accountancy Bodies and the Provision of Education and Training in Relation to Environmental Issues* (Edinburgh: ICAS).

Gray, R. H., Dillard, J. and Spence, C. (2009) Social accounting as if the world matters: an essay in postalgia and a new absurdism, *Public Management Review*, 11(5), pp. 545–573.

Gray, R. H., Owen, D. L. and Adams, C. (1996) *Accounting and Accountability: Changes and Challenges in Corporate Social and Environmental Reporting* (London: Prentice Hall).

Gray-Donald, J. and Selby, D. (Eds) (2008) *Green Frontiers: Environmental Educators Dancing Away from Mechanism* (Rotterdam: Sense Publishers).

Hazelton, J. and Haigh, M. (2010) Incorporating sustainability into the accounting curriculum: lessons learnt from an action research study, *Accounting Education: An International Journal*, 19(1/2), pp. 159–178.

Henriques, A. and Richardson, J. (2004) *The Triple Bottom Line: Does it Add Up?* (London: Earthscan).

Hippen, C., Yates, D., and Mason, K. (n.d.) *Ethnomethodology.* Available at http://www.umsl.edu/~keelr/3210/resources/Ethnomethodology.ppt (accessed 15 February 2010).

Hitchcock, D. and Willard, M. (2006) *The Business Guide to Sustainability: Practical Strategies and Tolls for Organisations* (London: Earthscan).

Hopwood, A. G. (2007) Whither accounting research?, *The Accounting Review*, 82(5), pp. 1356–1374.

Huckle, J. and Sterling, S. (1996) *Education for Sustainability* (London: Earthscan).

International Chamber of Commerce (1991) *Business Charter for Sustainable Development* (Paris: ICC).

Jackson, T. (2009) *Prosperity Without Growth? The Transition to a Sustainable Economy* (London: Sustainable Development Commission).

Jain, S. C. (Ed.) (2011) *Enhancing Global Competitiveness Through Sustainable Environmental Stewardship* (London: Edward Elgar).

Jones, P., Selby, D. and Sterling, S. (Eds) (2010) *Sustainability Education: Perspectives Across Higher Education* (London: Earthscan).

Kahn, R. and Kellner, D. (2007) Paulo Freire and Ivan Illich: technology, politics and the reconstruction of education, *Policy Futures in Education*, 5(4), pp. 431–448.

Kearins, K. and Springett, D. (2003) Educating for sustainability: developing critical skills, *Journal of Management Education*, 27(2), pp. 188–204.

Kelly, M. and Alam, M. (2009) Educating accounting students in the age of sustainability, *The Australian Accounting and Business & Finance Journal*, 3(4), pp. 30–44.

Kovel, J. (2002) *The Enemy of Nature: The End of Capitalism or the End of the World?* (London: Zed Books).

Laine, M. (2005) Meanings of the term 'sustainable development' in Finnish corporate disclosures, *Accounting Forum*, 29(4), pp. 395–413.

Laine, M. (2010) Towards sustaining the status quo: business talk of sustainability in Finnish corporate disclosures 1987–2005, *European Accounting Review*, 19(2), pp. 247–274.

Lewis, L., Humphrey, C. and Owen, D. (1992) Accounting and the social: a pedagogic perspective, *British Accounting Review*, 24(3), pp. 219–233.

Lockhart, J. A. and Mathews, M. R. (2000) Teaching environmental accounting: a four-part framework, *Advances in Accounting Education Teaching and Curriculum Innovations*, 3, pp. 57–84.

Lozano, R. (2006) Incorporation and institutionalization of SD into universities: breaking through barriers to change, *Journal of Cleaner Production*, 14, pp. 787–796.

Lucas, U. (2002) Uncertainties and contradictions: lecturers' conceptions of teaching introductory accounting, *British Accounting Review*, 34(2), pp. 183–204.

Lucas, U. (2008) Being 'pulled up short': creating moments of surprise and possibility in accounting education, *Critical Perspectives on Accounting*, 19(3), pp. 383–403.

Martin, S. (2011) 'Book review: *The Positive Deviant* by Sara Parkin', *HEA's ESD Project e-Newsletter*, 25 January, 4(3). Available at http://www.heacademy.ac.uk/ourwork/teachingandlearning/

Mathews, M. R. (1995) Social and environmental accounting: a practical demonstration of ethical concern? *Journal of Business Ethics*, 14, pp. 663–671.

Mathews, M. R. (2001) Some thoughts on social and environmental accounting education, *Accounting Education: An International Journal*, 10(4), pp. 335–352.

Mayhew, N. (1997) Fading to grey: the use and abuse of corporate executives' 'representational power', in: R. Welford (Ed.) *Hijacking Environmentalism: Corporate Response to Sustainable Development*, pp. 63–95 (London: Earthscan).

Mayper, A. G., Pavur, R. J., Merino, B. and Hoops, W. (2005) The impact of accounting education on ethical values: an institutional perspective, *Accounting in the Public Interest*, 5, pp. 32–55.

McPhail, K. (1999) The threat of ethical accountants: an application of Foucault's concept of ethics to accounting education and some thoughts on ethically educating for the other, *Critical Perspectives on Accounting*, 10(6), pp. 833–866.

McPhail, K. (2004) An emotional response to the state of accounting education: developing accounting students' emotional intelligence, *Critical Perspectives on Accounting*, 15, pp. 629–648.

Meadows, D. H., Meadows, D. L., Randers, J. and Behrens, W. H. (1972) *The Limits to Growth* (London: Pan).

Meadows, D. H., Randers, J. and Meadows, D. L. (2004) *The Limits to Growth: The 30-Year Update* (London: Earthscan).

Millennium Ecosystem Assessment (2005) *Living Beyond Our Means: Natural Assets and Human Well-Being: Statement from the Board.* Available at http://www.millenniumassessment.org/en/Products.BoardStatement

Milne, M. and Gray, R. H. (2007) Future prospects for corporate sustainability reporting, in: J. Unerman, J. Bebbington and B. O'Dwyer (Eds) *Sustainability Accounting and Accountability*, pp. 184–208 (London: Routledge).

Milne, M. J., Kearins, K. N. and Walton, S. (2006) Creating adventures in wonderland? The journey metaphor and environmental sustainability, *Organization*, 13(6), pp. 801–839.

Milne, M., Ball, A., and Gray, R. (2008) Wither ecology? The triple bottom line, the Global Reporting Initiative, and the institutionalization of corporate sustainability reporting. Paper presented to the American Accounting Association, Anaheim, August.

Milne, M. J., Tregigda, H. M. and Walton, S. (2009) Words not actions! The ideological role of sustainable development reporting, *Accounting Auditing and Accountability Journal*, 22(8), pp. 1211–1257.

Moneva, J. M., Archel, P. and Correa, C. (2006) GRI and the camouflaging of corporate unsustainability, *Accounting Forum*, 30(2), pp. 121–137.

Oberndorfer, M. (2004) *Sustainability Pays Off: An Analysis About the Stock Exchange Performance of Members of the World Business Council for Sustainable Development (WBCSD)* (Vienna: Kommunalkredit Dexia Asset Management).

Orlitsky, M., Schmidt, F. L. and Rynes, S. L. (2003) Corporate social and financial performance: a meta analysis, *Organization Studies*, 24(3), pp. 403–441.

Owen, D., Humphrey, C., and Lewis, L. (1994) *Social and Environmental Accounting Education in British Universities*, Certified Research Report No. 39 (London: ACCA).

Porritt, J. (2005) *Capitalism: As if the World Matters* (London: Earthscan).

Quinn, S., Gaughran, W. and Burke, S. (2009) Environmental sustainability in engineering education – quo vadis?, *International Journal of Sustainable Engineering*, 2(2), pp. 143–151.

Rands, G. P. and Starik, M. (2009) The short and glorious history of sustainability in North American management education, in: C. Wankel and J. A. F. Stoner (Eds) *Management Education for Global Sustainability*, pp. 19–49 (New York: IAP).

Rowe, A. L. and Wehrmeyer, W. (2010) Education for sustainability: developing MBA students' critical reflective and action learning in their work context, *Review of Business Research*, 10(2), pp. 145–149.

Rusinko, C. A. (2010) Integrating sustainability in management and business education: a matrix approach, *Academy of Management Learning & Education*, 9(3), pp. 507–519.

Rusinko, C. A. and Sama, L. M. (2009) Greening and sustainability across the management curriculum, *Journal of Management Education*, 33(3), pp. 271–275.

Schaltegger, S. and Wagner, M. (2006) *Managing the Business Case for Sustainability: An Integration of Social, Environmental and Economic Performance* (Sheffield: Greenleaf).

Shrivastava, P. (2010) Pedagogy of passion for sustainability, *Academy of Management Learning and Education*, 9(3), pp. 443–455.

Sipos, Y., Battisti, B. and Grimm, K. (2008) Achieving transformative sustainability learning: engaging head, hands and heart, *International Journal of Sustainability in Higher Education*, 9(1), pp. 68–86.

Sky (2012) *The Sustainable Generation: The Sky Future Leaders Study* (Middlesex: British Sky Broadcasting Group plc).

Spence, C. (2007) Social and environmental reporting and hegemonic discourse, *Accounting, Auditing & Accountability Journal*, 20(6), pp. 855–881.

Springett, D. (2005) 'Education for sustainability' in the business studies curriculum: a call for a critical agenda, *Business Strategy & the Environment*, 14(3), pp. 146–159.

Starik, M., Rands, G., Marcus, A. A. and Clark, T. S. (2010) From the guest editors: in search of sustainability in management education, *Academy of Management Learning and Education*, 9(3), pp. 377–383.

Stead, J. G. and Stead, W. E. (2010) Sustainability comes to management education and research: a story of coevolution, *Academy of Management Learning and Education*, 9(3), pp. 488–498.

Stevenson, L. (2002) Social and environmental accounting teaching in UK and Irish universities: a research note on changes between 1993 and 1998, *Accounting Education: An International Journal*, 11(4), pp. 331–346.

Stubbs, W. and Cocklin, C. (2008) Teaching sustainability to business students: shifting mindsets, *International Journal of Sustainability in Higher Education*, 9(3), pp. 208–221.

Swanson, D. L. (2005) Business ethics education at bay: addressing a crisis of legitimacy, *Issues in Accounting Education*, 20(3), pp. 247–253.

Thielemann, U. (2000) A brief theory of the market – ethically focused, *International Journal of Social Economics*, 27(1), pp. 6–31.

Thomas, T. E. (2005) Are business students buying it? A theoretical framework for measuring attitudes toward the legitimacy of environmental sustainability, *Business Strategy & the Environment*, 14(3), pp. 186–197.

Thomson, I. (2007) Mapping the terrain of sustainability accounting, in: J. Unerman, J. Bebbington, and B. O'Dwyer (Eds.), *Sustainability Accounting and Accountability*, pp. 19–36 (London: Routledge).

Thomson, I. and Bebbington, J. (2004) It doesn't matter what you teach? *Critical Perspectives on Accounting*, 15(4–5), pp. 609–628.

Thomson, I. and Bebbington, J. (2005) Social and environmental reporting in the UK: a pedagogic evaluation, *Critical Perspectives on Accounting*, 16(5), pp. 507–533.

Thorpe, J. and Prakash-Mani, K. (2003) Developing value: the business case for sustainability in emerging markets, *Greener Management International*, 44 (Special Issue on Sustainability Performance and Business Competitiveness), pp. 17–32.

Tilbury, D. (2011) Higher education for sustainability: a global overview of commitment and progress, in: Global University Network for Innovation (GUNI) (Ed.), *Higher Education's Commitment to Sustainability: From Understanding to Action*, pp. 1–21 (Paris: Palgrave Macmillan).

Tregidga, H. M. and Milne, M. J. (2006) From sustainable management to sustainable development: a longitudinal analysis of a leading New Zealand environmental reporter, *Business Strategy and the Environment*, 15(4), pp. 219–241.

Turner, R. K. (Ed.) (1993) *Sustainable Environmental Management: Principles and Practice* (London: Belhaven Press).

UNESCO (2011) *Education for Sustainable Development: An Expert Review of Processes and Learning* (Paris: UNESCO).

United Nations Development Programme (UNDP) (2010) *Human Development Report 2010*. Available at http://hdr.undp.org/en/reports/global/hdr2010/chapters/en/

United Nations Environment Programme (UNEP) (2002) *Global Environmental Outlook (GEO – 3) 2002* (London: Earthscan).

United Nations World Commission on Environment and Development (WCED) (1987) *Our Common Future (The Brundtland Report)* (Oxford: OUP).

Walck, C. (2009) Integrating sustainability into management education, *Journal of Management Education*, 33(3), pp. 384–390.

Weizsäcker, E. Von, Lovins, A. B. and Lovins, L. H. (1997) *Factor Four: Doubling Wealth, Halving Resource Use* (London: Earthscan).

Whiting, V., de Pillis, E. and Hatch, J. (2011) A five-phase approach to poverty eradication: an educational proposal for sustainable leadership and sustainable development, *Journal of Corporate Citizenship*, 39(December), pp. 41–57.

Wilhelm, W. B. (2008) Marketing education for sustainability, *Journal for Advancement of Marketing Education*, 13, pp. 8–20.

World Business Council for Sustainable Development (WBCSD) (2002) The business case for sustainable development, February. Available at http://www.wbcsd.org

World Business Council for Sustainable Development (WBCSD) (2011) *People Matter, Engage*, World Business Council for Sustainable Development. Available at http://www.wbcsd.org/DocRoot/neOrafZJodvnX2ifhblq/People%20Matter%20Engage.pdf

WWF (2004) *Living Planet Report 2004* (Gland, Switzerland: WWF – World Wide Fund for Nature).

WWF (2008) *Living Planet Report 2008* (Gland, Switzerland: WWF – World Wide Fund for Nature).

York, R., Rosa, E. A. and Dietz, T. (2003) Footprints on the Earth: the environmental consequences of modernity, *American Sociological Review*, 68(2), pp. 279–300.

Zimmerman, M. E. (1994) *Contesting Earth's Future: Radical Ecology and Postmodernity* (London: University of California Press).

Appendix: A Selection of the Reading Required for the Module

- Gray, Owen, and Adams. (1996) *Accounting and Accountability* (London: Prentice Hall).
- Porritt, J. (2005) *Capitalism as if the World Matters* (London: Earthscan).
- Bakan, J. (2004) *The Corporation: The Pathological Pursuit of Profit and Power* (London: Constable and Robinson).
- Jacobson, R. (1991) Economic efficiency and the quality of life, *Journal of Business Ethics*, 10, pp. 201–209.
- Thielemann, U. (2000) A brief theory of the market – ethically focused, *International Journal of Social Economics*, 27(1), pp. 6–31.

- Lehman, G. (1999) Disclosing new worlds: a role for social and environmental accounting and auditing, *Accounting Organizations and Society*, 24(3), pp. 217–242.
- Mintzberg, H. (1983) The case for corporate social responsibility, *The Journal of Business Strategy*, 4(2), pp. 3–15.
- Doane, D. (2005) The myth of CSR, *Stanford Social Innovation Review*. Available at http://www.ssireview.com/pdf/2005FA_Feature_Doane.pdf
- Tilston, N. (2004) CSR doesn't matter – business profits do, in: *The Changing Role of Business in Society: Ashridge Best MBA Essay Award 2004* (London: ACCA).
- Milne, M. and Gray, R. H. (2007) Future prospects for sustainability reporting, in: J. Unerman, J. Bebbington, and B. O'Dwyer (Eds.), *Sustainability Accounting and Accountability*, ch. 10 (London: Routledge).
- Gray, R. H. and Milne, M. (2004) Towards reporting on the triple bottom line: mirages, methods and myths, in: A. Henriques and J. Richardson (Eds.), *The Triple Bottom Line: Does it All Add Up?*, pp. 70–80 (London: Earthscan).
- Frederick, W. C. (1986) Towards CSR3: why ethical analysis is indispensable and unavoidable in corporate affairs, *California Management Review*, 28(2), pp. 126–141.
- O'Dwyer, B. (2003) Conceptions of corporate social responsibility: the nature of managerial capture, *Accounting Auditing and Accountability Journal*, 16(4), pp. 523–557.
- Gray, R. H. (2006) Does sustainability reporting improve corporate behaviour? Wrong question? Right time?, *Accounting and Business Research*, 36, pp. 65–88.
- Murray, A., Sinclair, D., Power, D., and Gray, R. (2006) Do financial markets care about social and environmental disclosure? Further evidence and exploration from the UK, *Accounting, Auditing and Accountability Journal*, 19(2), pp. 228–255.
- Ullmann, A. E. (1985) Data in search of a theory: a critical examination of the relationships among social performance, social disclosure and economic performance of US firms, *Academy of Management Review*, 10(3), pp. 540–557.
- KPMG International Surveys of R + Sustain Ability/UNEP reports.
- Wally, N. and Whitehead, B. (1994) It's not easy being green, *Harvard Business Review*, pp. 46–52 + Various authors (1994) The challenge of going green, *Harvard Business Review*, pp. 37–50.
- Gray, R. H. and Bebbington, K. J. (2000) Environmental accounting, managerialism and sustainability: is the planet safe in the hands of business and accounting?, *Advances in Environmental Accounting and Management*, 1, pp. 1–44.
- Gray, R. H., Bebbington, K. J., Walters, D., and Thomson, I. (1995) The greening of enterprise: an exploration of the (non) role of environmental accounting and environmental accountants in organisational change, *Critical Perspectives on Accounting*, 6(3), pp. 211–239.
- Owen, D. L. (1990) Towards a theory of social investment: a review essay, *Accounting, Organisations and Society*, 15(3), pp. 249–266.
- Kreander, N. (2001) *An Analysis of European Ethical Funds*, Research Paper No. 33 (London: ACCA).
- Kreander, N., Gray, R. H., Power, D. M., and Sinclair, C. D. (2005) Evaluating the performance of ethical and non-ethical funds: a matched pair analysis, *Journal of Business Finance and Accounting*, 32(7/8), pp. 1465–1493.
- Gray, R. H. (2000) Current developments and trends in social and environmental auditing, reporting and attestation: a review and comment, *International Journal of Auditing*, pp. 247–268.
- Medawar, C. (1976) The social audit: a political view, *Accounting, Organisations and Society*, 1(4), pp. 389–394.

- Harte, G. and Owen D. L. (1987) Fighting de-industrialisation: the role of local government social audits, *Accounting, Organisations and Society*, 12(2), pp. 123–142.
- Owen, D. L., Swift, T., Bowerman, M., and Humphreys, C. (2000) The new social audits: accountability, managerial capture or the agenda of social champions?, *European Accounting Review*, 9(1), pp. 81–98.
- Adams, C. (2004) The ethical, social and environmental reporting-performance portrayal gap, *Accounting, Auditing and Accountability Journal*, 17(5), pp. 731–757.
- Gray, R. H., Dey, C., Owen, D., Evans, R., and Zadek, S. (1997) Struggling with the praxis of social accounting: stakeholders, accountability, audits and procedures, *Accounting, Auditing and Accountability Journal*, 10(3), pp. 325–364.
- Henriques, A. and Richardson, J. (2004) *The Triple Bottom Line: Does it Add Up?* (London: Earthscan).

me with a one-page reflection to share their thoughts: what they consider to be important, complex, strange, simplistic or otherwise intriguing in the text. Further, what I always emphasize is that there are neither right nor wrong answers; only intellectual laziness is not tolerated (see Gray, 2013). Similarly, throughout the course, value is given to high-quality argumentation, reasoning and respectful dialogue. Contrary to Gray (2013), however, I find it useful to include feelings within the permitted range of expressions, since this helps to bring out the students' humanity. Some students have difficulty entering a fact-based debate on these complex topics; expressing one's thoughts via fear, anger and joy may create a pathway through which discussions can be entered.

Hines (1988) usually works exceptionally well, since (on the surface) it is not only accessible, but also provides numerous challenges to the fundamental assumptions in accounting education. These reflections and the subsequent class discussion lay the foundation for my class. I seek to contest accounting as the students know it, to bring forth (some of) the hidden assumptions underlying both their own thinking and the accounting education in the university. My main aims are: first, to show the students that there is something seriously wrong in our societies, and then to highlight that 'neutral and benign' accounting is intrinsically linked with sustainability. Or, as one student put it, *'the course sought to disprove everything we had been taught of accounting'* (Student feedback). In hindsight, it is indeed stunning that from day one I have practically had complete freedom regarding which topics I would include and how I would teach them in my course.

Even though, on a personal level, I am very critical of the discourse of sustainable business, I have come to conclude that offering doomsday prophecies and extremist solutions only alienate the students. Accounting students who are willing to learn about social and environmental issues are far too valuable to be frightened away. Nevertheless, the main aims in my teaching include building criticality towards organizational discourses, creating awareness of the inherent conflicts and debunking the perceived objectivity of accounting. Simultaneously, I consider it important to help the students feel empowered, meaning that they need to feel that there are things that they can do as individuals. I feel that, in the class, there needs to be a strong connection to both the local and personal perspectives. Hence, building from something that students experience on a regular basis, like food, local traffic and everyday consumption, facilitates the creation of a dialogic atmosphere. From there, it is easier to question the institutionalized beliefs and matters that are taken for granted.

As a concluding remark, I wish to note that reading Gray's take on teaching was a puzzling experience, since I found alignment in my own thinking almost throughout the text. Yet, where I diverge is that I would rather ensure that everyone sleeps at night. We, as citizens, teachers or students, must do what we can, and we can do a lot more if we have slept well. Further, I feel that during my 10 or so years as an accounting teacher, both the social context and the participating students have changed. The students appear to be increasingly sceptical of the accounting curriculum and worldview that it promotes. Consequently, feedback such as the following may become more frequent in the future:

> Thank you once more for the course, [which] had a very significant role in my life. Never give up hope! (Student feedback)

References

Gray, R. H. (2013) Sustainability and accounting education: the elephant in the classroom, *Accounting Education: An International Journal*, 22(4), pp. 308–332.

Gray, R. and Collison, D. (2002) Can't see the wood for the trees, can't see the trees for the numbers? Accounting education, sustainability and the public interest, *Critical Perspectives on Accounting*, 13, pp. 797–836.

Hines, R. D. (1988) Financial accounting: in communicating reality, we construct reality, *Accounting, Organisations and Society*, 13(3), pp. 251–261.

Thomson, I. and Bebbington, J. (2004) It doesn't matter what you teach? *Critical Perspectives on Accounting*, 15(4–5), pp. 609–628.

conventional accounting education. A significant, though not necessarily extensive, body of research has sought to investigate, discuss and reflect on 'how' and 'why' social and environmental accounting topics have been (or not been) introduced in educational programmes (Collison, Ferguson and Stevenson, 2007). This research provided insights to enhance academic understanding of the complexities, difficulties and controversies arising when teaching social and environmental responsibilities. Nevertheless, as brilliantly noted by Gray, the existing literature mainly concentrates on accounting education *about* sustainability, rather than accounting education *for (pro)* sustainability, which is an accounting education that embraces and meets the challenges and conflicts posed by sustainability (Bebbington, O'Dwyer and Unerman, 2007). What is lacking is an accounting education (and accounting) which is 'at the service of' (i.e. functional to) the urgent and important demands of sustainability, which 'embraces life and death' issues (Gray, 2013, p. 323). An accounting education *for (pro)* sustainability should:

1. introduce, discuss and reflect on the (scary) data and problems we are exposed to when we are confronted with (un)sustainability, e.g. climate change; starvation; inequality and human rights exploitation; and
2. be 'transformative' (Thomson and Bebbington, 2005) in how students understand, acquire awareness of and (at least potentially) act in their individual or social undertakings to address these issues.

Gray reflects on an educational engagement experiment where the complex issues surrounding sustainability were dealt with in an undergraduate module at the University of St Andrews. Gray's paper makes a valuable contribution by providing empirical insights into understanding how to bring the 'cold wind of sustainability' into classrooms and deal with concerns that should 'keep [all of us] awake at night' (Gray, 2013, p. 318). This Commentary presents the result of a dialectic engagement with these issues and is less about this fascinating paper per se, but are my thoughts and reflections on the challenges raised; in particular, the pivotal role that AE4S can (and should) play as 'utopic' pedagogy (Bimbi, 2002, in referring to Freire) and the design of accounting *for* sustainability modules and courses.

It is my contention that the ultimate purpose of accounting education *for* sustainability is to assist students in 'consciousness-reaching' (Freire, 2002) of the (un)sustainable state of our current economic-socio-cultural systems. Accounting education *for* sustainability should fundamentally be a pedagogy of, and for, those who are (or will be) 'oppressed' (Freire, 2002) by 'a-sustainable' and/or 'un-sustainable' modes of thinking and living. 'Oppressed' is used to indicate someone who lives in a physical or intellectual state of *'pre-', 'a-'* and/or *'un-' consciousness* of the (un)sustainability status that results in 'oppressing and suffocating' (Freire, 2002) their personal and social existence. Accounting education *for* sustainability should (and can) represent a *utopic* pedagogy, the final purpose of which is to 'free' those who are oppressed by 'a-sustainability' and/or 'un-sustainability' in order to reach a state of 'critical conscience' as *a sine qua non* for 'transformative praxis' (Thomson and Bebbington, 2005). The notion of 'utopia' is used to indicate the 'indissoluble union' 'between *denouncing* and *announcing*' (Bimbi, 2002, p. 15, emphasis added). 'Denouncing and announcing', which derive from the Latin word 'nuntiare', meaning to 'proclaim', are used in their etymological sense to mean, respectively, the activities of '*de*-nuntiare' (i.e. condemning) and '*ad*-nuntiare'(i.e. bringing or adding novelties). Accounting education *for* sustainability may become a means of liberation and consciousness-reaching only if it is able to be 'utopic', that is if it is able to conjugate *denunciation* (severe criticism) with *announcement* (constructive proposal).

From this perspective, therefore, accounting education *for* sustainability should create 'cognitive dissonance' and 'intellectual disruptiveness', facilitating 'substantive reflective analysis' (Gray, 2013, p. 320), but simultaneously enabling the emergence of transcendent concrete actions/initiatives. Paraphrasing Freire, accounting education *for* sustainability should promote the process of 'consciousness-reaching' as a *sine qua non* for 'transformative praxis' i.e. the dialectical synthesis of critical reflection and action (Thomson and Bebbington, 2005). It is only through reflection-grounded action that transformative change towards less unsustainable modes of acting and living can be achieved. The search for transformative praxis requires '*passion*' for the issues at stake. It is difficult to imagine a transformative praxis without 'passion'. To have passion means to mentally and emotionally engage *with*, and act *for*, something you really care about and 'keep[s] you awake at night' (Gray, 2013, p. 318).

The design of modules and courses of accounting *for* sustainability should encourage students to achieve an informed understanding of the issues as *a sine qua non* for passion-led actions. To do this, these modules and courses should describe and introduce the 'elephant' to students in a familiar and understandable fashion using their everyday experiences and visibilities. Students need to be placed in situations as if confronted directly by these issues vis-à-vis practical and palpable problems to which they can relate. Modules should encourage students to explicitly address, along with meta-questions about the sustainability of the planet and mankind, questions such as:

- What are the implications of the (un)sustainability for me, my family, the community in which I live, my country, etc.?
- What are the causes of the status quo?
- What may I do in my everyday life to contribute to find solutions, if anything?

By reducing the distance between everyday life and the complex issues of (un)-sustainability, the 'elephant' may be perceived as being something familiar with which to engage *with* and act *for*. Creating this 'closeness' to sustainability is critical to enabling passion-grounded praxis. Such modules and courses should be designed to promote a constant dialogue with and between students and encourage critical confrontation through the emergence of diverse views supported by data, linked to everyday examples and part of a search for practical solutions.

A wide range of teaching methods are needed to create confrontational realistic contexts. These might include: conventional theory lectures, active tutorials/workshop, movies and documentaries; role plays; site visits to organisations that have adopted social and environmental responsible practices; classes in alternative settings, e.g. in a forest or park; practical community/business developmental projects; and events to disseminate these experiences. The underlying intention is to encourage:

(a) critical understanding of the issues related to sustainability;
(b) problematization in order to identify the peculiarities of specific problems; and
(c) the search for actual, even if partial, solutions to address the limit situations.

However, one cannot be too prescriptive and should allow the educator flexibility to adapt to their teaching context (e.g. teaching accounting for sustainability at the University of St Andrews is very different to teaching at the University of Bergamo).

If we wish to have an accounting education *for* sustainability that is 'transformative', then it should be *utopic* (i.e. disruptive and constructive), praxis-grounded and passion-driven. This requires a fundamental re-think of teaching systems as well as the role of schools and universities as centres for 'transformative changes' within society, business and communities. Whether or not this would be enough to get the 'elephant' in all our room(s) is debatable, but not being able to do more does not preclude the possibility of dreaming about what we wish to do but can't do. Nor does it preclude imagining what we could do but haven't done yet. If we are to stay awake at night we should dream of better futures as well as our nightmares.

References

Bebbington, J., O'Dwyer, B. and Unerman, J. (2007) Postscript and conclusions, in: J. Unerman, J. Bebbington and B. O'Dwyer (Eds) *Sustainability Accounting and Accountability*, pp. 345–349 (London: Routledge).

Bimbi, L. (2002) Prefazione alla nuova edizione italiana de 'La pedagogia degli oppressi' di Paulo Freire, in: P. Freire, *La pedagogia degli oppressi* (Torino: EGA).

Collison, D., Ferguson, J. and Stevenson, L. (2007) Sustainability accounting and education, in: J. Unerman, J. Bebbington and B. O'Dwyer (Eds) *Sustainability Accounting and Accountability*, pp. 327–344 (London: Routledge).

Freire, P. (2002) *La pedagogia degli oppressi* (Torino: EGA). (Italian translation of the *Pedagogia do oprimido*).

Gray, R. (2013) Sustainability and accounting education: the elephant in the classroom, *Accounting Education: an international journal*, 22(4), pp. 308–332.

Thomson, I. (2007) Mapping the terrain of sustainability accounting, in: J. Unerman, J. Bebbington and B. O'Dwyer (Eds) *Sustainability Accounting and Accountability*, pp. 19–36 (London: Routledge).

Thomson, I. and Bebbington, J. (2005) Social and environmental reporting in the UK: a pedagogic evaluation, *Critical Perspectives on Accounting*, 16(5), pp. 507–533.

Accountants (FEE), and large global accountancy firms such as Deloittes, Ernst and Young, KPMG, and PwC. Organisations that have already adopted an integrated approach to financial reporting include BASF, Bloomberg, BT, Phillips, Novo Nordisk, United Technologies Corporation (UTC) and American Electric Power (AEP). The Association of Chartered Certified Accountants (ACCA) has also produced its first integrated report for the 2011–2012 period (ACCA, 2012a).

The above and other organisations are expressing the view that integrated reports may provide a more holistic, multi-dimensional and lucid representation of the business than the current reporting model, which has a greater focus on detailed historical financial information.

In a news release (ACCA, 2011), Richard Martin (Head of Financial Reporting at ACCA) commented on the aspirations that critics of the current model have expressed, as follows:

> Many critics of the current reporting framework have called for change which encourages companies to give readers of their accounts "the bigger picture" of how they are doing and better quality information about how they are achieving value and managing the challenges they face over the long term as well as the short term.

IR has been defined in several source documents, but it is defined by the IIRC as follows:

> Integrated Reporting brings together the material information about an organization's strategy, governance, performance and prospects in a way that reflects the commercial, social and environmental context within which it operates. (IIRC, 2011, p. 3)

IR has also been referred to as 'One Report' (Eccles and Krzus, 2010). This name implies that IR provides information on financial and non-financial performance in a single document, showing the relationship between financial and non-financial performance and how these inter-related dimensions are creating or destroying value for shareholders and other stakeholders.

The above organisations and business opinion leaders suggest that IR may provide a richer picture of the organisation. This would be achieved by drawing from a wider range of sources of information than the current reporting model, which would include both qualitative as well as quantitative data to offer a clearer insight into a business, about how well the organisation is managed, and whether it is performing sustainably.

The increased prominence and recognition of IR globally could have significant implications for accounting education, both for professional qualifications and university accounting curricula. These implications may include changes to the traditional structure of accounting programmes and how they are assessed. More prominence may be given to certain subject areas (such as strategy, governance, risk and performance, and financial management) and a greater emphasis may be required on the synthesis of some of the key accounting disciplines. As far as assessment is concerned, more extensive use may need to be made of the integrated case study approach and of other integrated approaches to assessment. Finally, a greater emphasis may need to be given to strategic, qualitative and non-financial considerations in the assessment and reporting of corporate performance and business outlook.

2. Structure of the Paper

This paper is structured in the following way.

- Section 3 will begin with a discussion of the origins of IR from *The Corporate Report* and the emergence of corporate social responsibility (CSR) and such related concepts as 'green' accounting, sustainability reporting, environmental accounting and triple bottom line accounting (TBL).

- Section 4 focuses on the recent developments and initiatives specifically relating to IR, starting with Accounting for Sustainability (A4S), the Global Reporting Initiative (GRI) and guidance within the FEE Fact Sheets.
- Section 5 focuses on publications underpinning the main proposals for IR. These include: the IFAC consultation paper *Competent and Versatile: How Professional Accountants Drive Sustainable Organizational Success*; the IFAC *Sustainability Framework 2* (2011) discussion paper; the IFRS *Management Commentary* (IASB, 2010a); and the International Auditing and Assurance Standards Board (IAASB) discussion paper (2011).
- Sections 6 and 7 explore in more detail the main content of two key papers on IR; the IIRC report *Towards Integrated Reporting – Communicating Value in the 21st Century* and the South African discussion paper (2011) *A Framework for Integrated Reporting and the Integrated Report* published by the IRC, both of which include recommendations about the key elements to be addressed in an integrated report.
- Section 8 then considers the implication of a greater emphasis on IR for professional and university accounting education and on the content and structure of the accounting curriculum in the twenty-first century. This leads to a synthesis of the main recommendations contained within the key reports on IR into six key outcomes or elements, to be included within a modern professional accounting curriculum.
- Section 9 of the paper examines how ACCA, as a longstanding global sponsor and supporter of sustainability and CSR, embeds outcomes relating to the wider reporting responsibilities of the IR model within its qualification curriculum.
- The final section (Section 10) suggests where possible future accounting curriculum development may be focused, to ensure professional and university accounting qualifications remain fully aligned with IR requirements beyond 2012.

3. Origins of Integrated Reporting

IR is not an entirely new approach. As long ago as the 1970s, a more integrated and balanced approach to corporate reporting was recommended. The landmark publication, *The Corporate Report*, published by the UK Accounting Standards Steering Committee (1975), questioned the narrow shareholder and stewardship perspective taken at that time by accountants and directors in reporting the performance of companies. *The Corporate Report* emphasised the need for a 'user' perspective rather than the 'shareholder' or financial 'stewardship' perspective that emerged as the traditional agency model for limited companies. This was originally highlighted by Smith (1776), on the basis that the operation of a limited company entails a separation of ownership and control:

> The directors of such [joint-stock] companies, however, being the managers rather of other people's money than of their own, it cannot well be expected, that they should watch over it with the same anxious vigilance with which the partners in a private co-partnery frequently watch over their own. (Smith 1776/1937, p. 700)

The Corporate Report, however, implied as early as the 1970s that the board of directors should act as the 'agents' of and be accountable to a wider range of principals than shareholders, who were traditionally the main focus under the narrower 'stewardship' perspective as envisaged under the agency perspective considered by Adam Smith. *The Corporate Report* therefore recommended a wider view of accountability where lenders, employees, customers, suppliers, the local community and even the general public were recognised as having legitimate rights to published information.

Gray, Owen and Adams (1996) argued that there is a range of positions that companies, or, more specifically, their directors, can take to accountability and more specifically to CSR. These move from a 'pristine capitalist' view, which regards the company as only having a responsibility to maximise shareholder wealth, to 'deep ecologists', which assert that the company has no intrinsic ownership rights over any resources and that it should operate sustainably and be future-oriented. They explained that the degree of CSR and the type of reporting that supports this depends mainly on the agency perspective that the business (specifically its directors) takes towards its responsibilities and obligations. They suggested that corporate reports needed to adopt a wider position on responsibility and accountability and move away from one based on a narrow fiduciary perspective, where the scope of the reporting function would be limited to the preparation of financial reports, relating mainly to the recognition and measurement of shareholder income and wealth.

Such a view suggests that 'separation of ownership and control', where the view of agency is broader, needs to be re-phrased. Under a broader agency position it may be more relevant to consider the separation of 'stakeholder claims' and 'corporate responsibility for resources and their potential economic, social and environmental impacts'.

Mendelow (1991) and Mitchell, Agle and Wood (1997), amongst others, have since attempted to map these stakeholder groups or 'users' according to varying degrees of power and interest in the business, taking into account the legitimacy and urgency of the stakeholders' claims on the organisation. Such an analysis can also assist preparers of integrated reports to decide who needs to know what and by when. An example of this was a case study undertaken by Gray *et al.* (1997) of Traidcraft, a small company that encouraged fair trade between developing and developed nations and prepared a 'social account' as part of its corporate report, based on an analysis of stakeholder rights and interests, identified and prioritised according to their needs and importance.

The process of stakeholder mapping or prioritising is inevitably dependent upon the social, political and economic priorities and perspectives of the organisations producing corporate reports. In considering the prioritisation of stakeholder power and interest further, Cooper and Owen (2007) analysed a framework for examining the relationship between CSR and organisational financial performance. Their paper suggests that some ambiguity in any empirical research findings may arise from the varying ability and motivation of managers to prioritise their social responsibility initiatives for stakeholders with power, urgency and legitimacy, and the relative ability of these stakeholders to reward or punish the entity based on their evaluations of the entity's activity or impacts.

In terms of how standard setting agencies have viewed financial reporting obligations, some regulatory bodies have promoted the reporting of more qualitative and forward-facing information rather than relying too much on 'historical' quantitative information. In 1993 the UK Accounting Standards Board (ASB) recognised the need for recommendations relating to more narrative information as contained in an operating and financial report (OFR) as part of the Directors' Report. OFR regulations were passed into company law in the UK in 2005 and published Reporting Standard 1 (2006a), which required companies to give a broad view of the performance and impact of a company's activity. However, the statutory requirement for the OFR and RS1 was withdrawn in the UK later in that year, although the ASB later introduced a *Reporting Statement of Best Practice* (2006b) as guidance on what to include in such a report. The main components suggested for such a report were a review of the nature, objectives and strategies of the business, the current and future development, and performance, resources, risks and uncertainties, relationships and financial position. The guidance also included recommendations about the reporting of key performance indicators and other useful measures.

During the 1970s, 1980s and 1990s, other approaches to financial reporting were proposed and supported. These included CSR, 'sustainability' accounting, (Unerman, Bebbington and O'Dwyer, 2007), environmental or 'green accounting' (Owen, Gray and Bebbington, 1997), and Triple Bottom Line (TBL) accounting (Elkington, 2004). The term 'sustainability accounting' has often been used interchangeably with CSR and the TBL headings of *economic viability*, *social responsibility* and *environmental responsibility*.

Under sustainability accounting the economic impact reported in a sustainability report might include the impact on local employment and living standards as a consequence of the organisation's operations. The social impact might include employee terms and conditions or the level of social investment or interaction between the company and the community. The environmental impact might include the quality of waste water discharged or the level of greenhouse gas emissions from operations.

While environmental considerations are often the main focus of attention in sustainability reports, the TBL definition of sustainability is a broader concept. In addition to preservation of the physical environment and stewardship of natural resources, sustainability considers the economic and social context of doing business and also encompasses the business systems, models and behaviours necessary for long-term value creation, while preserving or maintaining capital as defined from economic, social and environmental perspectives.

Specifically, TBL suggested that companies should prepare three different (and quite separate) bottom lines, based on the three Ps: a traditional 'profit account'; a 'people account' of how socially responsible an organisation is; and the company's 'planet account', or how environmentally responsible it has been.

While environmental, 'green', sustainability or TBL accounting focus on both the external accountability mechanism (financial reporting) and on providing an assessment and managing the social and environmental costs and impacts of the company's operation (management accounting), other aspects, such as strategic outlook, governance issues and key risk analysis, were much less prominent in such reporting models.

4. Recent Integrated Reporting Initiatives

In December 2009, the Prince of Wales sponsored an Accounting for Sustainability forum (A4S), which convened a high level meeting of investors, standard setters, companies, accountancy bodies, and UN representatives. These organisations collaborated with the GRI, founded in 1997, and supported by the United Nations Environment Programme (UNEP), to promote economic sustainability. This collaboration resulted in the creation of a completely new body, known as the International Integrated Reporting Committee (IIRC), which was formally announced in August 2010.

This body was tasked with building upon the GRI framework to develop proposals for an IR framework that was to be taken to the G20 meeting held in November 2011. A discussion paper was also been published in South Africa, entitled *A Framework for Integrated Reporting and the Integrated Report*, in January 2011.

The GRI framework developed four sets of guidelines relating to IR. The GRI issued a *G3 Sustainability Reporting Framework* (2006), drawing upon principles included in the IFAC *Conceptual Framework for Financial Reporting* (2010), widening its application to include sustainability issues. GRI are currently developing a G4 or 4th generation of guidelines, planned for publication in 2013.

The GRI G3 guidelines include principles to define report content regarding stakeholder inclusiveness, sustainability context and completeness. There are also qualitative characteristics relating to report quality, such as balance, comparability, accuracy, timeliness, reliability and clarity. Finally, there is guidance on how to set the report's boundaries in terms of reporting on the basis of materiality of impact and the level of influence, or control, over reporting entities.

These guidelines expect company reports to include coverage of business strategy objectives, the company profile, the management approach, and a list of key performance indicators.

Following from the publication of these guidelines, The Federation of European Accountants (FEE) issued an updated fact sheet (2012), which contains key messages in response to the IIRC. According to the FEE Fact Sheet (2012), the principles underpinning integrated reports are that they should be about taking a holistic approach to enable investors and other stakeholders to understand how an organisation is really performing, addressing the wider as well as the longer-term impact of decisions and actions.

The Fact Sheet suggests that there should be connectivity and linkage between information reported on and information required about the impact of resource usage and emissions on core business and sustainability along the business value chain. The commentary should include a considered and well-supported view of prospective performance, taking into account strategic environmental and market issues to allow a meaningful comparison of plans with achievements. Consistent with principles of TBL (Elkington, 2004), integrated reports should therefore use much more from internal management information as a basis for the external reports. It is also crucial that information produced in an integrated report should be trustworthy, reliable and capable of being independently verified.

This requirement introduces additional challenges for auditors, as will be discussed in the next section.

The FEE Fact Sheet also recommends that integrated reports should be flexible, to allow them to evolve, reflecting changes in reporting requirements, and should ultimately act as a catalyst for behavioural change within the business.

5. IFAC Background Papers on Integrated Reporting

Building on the broad principles within the IFAC *Conceptual Framework* (2010), and as background to more specific work on IR models published by other bodies subsequently, the IFAC has issued several background papers on the framework and practice of sustainable financial reporting. These refer to both accounting and auditing issues and implications. To place IR in a wider context, IFAC issued a consultation paper (2010), which identified the roles of professional accountants in business and then identified eight drivers of sustainable organisations that should be reported upon. The accountants' roles were described as *creators of value, enablers of value, preservers of value* and *reporters of value*. These labels summarise the role of the accountant as sustainably creating, supporting and reporting value for the business. The eight key drivers of sustainability relating to these roles were identified as follows:

- customer and stakeholder focus;
- effective leadership and strategy;
- integrated governance, risk and control;
- innovation and adaptability;
- financial management;

- people and talent management;
- strategy execution; and
- effective and transparent communication.

As can be seen from this list, the drivers widen the scope of financial reporting to include long-term sustainable performance and other factors such as strategy and innovation, governance, risk and control and stakeholder relationship management, in addition to financial performance appraisal.

To complement the above consultation paper, IFAC's International Accounting Standards Board (IASB) published a *Practice Statement* (2010b), which provided a framework for the presentation of management commentary. This statement outlined the purpose, principles and presentation of such information. The main elements of this paper included commentary on the nature of the business, objectives and strategies, resources, risks and relationships, results and prospects, and performance measures and indicators. The International Auditing and Assurance Standards Board (IAASB) of IFAC also produced a discussion paper (2011), which dealt with the audit implications of increased subjectivity introduced in IR. This, they argued, increases through a potential 'blurring of boundaries' as more narrative and prospective information is included and through the inclusion of much more qualitative rather than quantitative information.

Following the above publications, IFAC also produced a *Sustainability Framework 2.0* (2011), which focused on three broad perspectives for IR: the business strategy perspective; the operational perspective; and the reporting perspective. Within the strategy perspective the suggested content of integrated reports includes such areas as vision and leadership, stakeholder engagement, goal setting and risk management. The operational perspective focuses on performance management and sustainability issues, including waste management and carbon footprinting. Finally, the reporting perspective addresses organisational reporting strategies, sustainability impacts, and enhanced transparency through additional narrative reporting, within materiality thresholds.

All of the above statements, discussion papers, guidelines and frameworks effectively recommend the inclusion of more strategic, forward-facing and relevant information for decision-making or support purposes, as compared with the traditional stewardship reporting model.

To emphasise the decision-support role of integrated financial reporting, and the broader base of stakeholders for whom IR is intended, the concept of the 'greatest shareholder' as a user of such reports is described in the IFAC framework paper as follows:

> The greatest shareholder today is no longer the wealthy family, but it is the individual via his or her financial institution and pension fund. The same individual is also the employee of the company; the customer who chooses between the products of company A or company B; the voter for the government of the day and for the trustee of the pension fund. In addition, the individual is also a citizen of a country who expects his or her neighbor to act as a decent citizen, and as a consequence today, the individual citizen expects the corporate citizen to act as a decent citizen. (Mervyn King, Chairman, International Integrated Reporting Committee)

6. Towards Integrated Reporting

In 2011 the International Integrated Reporting Committee (IIRC) brought together world leaders from the corporate, investment, accounting, securities, regulatory, academic, civil

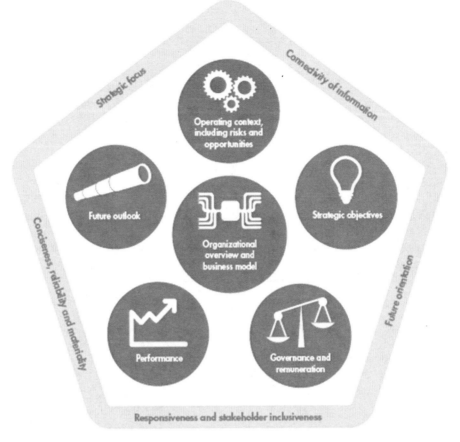

Figure 1. An international integrated reporting framework.
Source: *The IIRC Draft Discussion Paper* (2013, p. 7). Copyright © 2013 by the International Integrated Reporting Council. All rights reserved. Used with permission of the International Integrated Reporting Council. Permission is granted to make copies of this work to achieve maximum exposure and feedback.

society and standard setting sectors to develop a new IR framework, with clear proposals for the content of such reports.

As a result of this, and drawing upon material within the background papers included in the previous section, the IIRC published a discussion paper, *Towards Integrated Reporting: Communicating Value in the 21st Century*.

Figure 1 shows the main components of an integrated report, as taken from the IIRC (2011) paper.

The six main components shown in the IIRC Framework are underpinned by five guiding principles, which are that the reports should have a strategic focus, that there should be a connectivity of information, that the information presented should be future-oriented, based on responsiveness and stakeholder inclusiveness and concise, reliable and material.

As can be seen from Figure 1, the main headings and principles in this framework overlap considerably with many of the headings used within earlier work, notably the OFR and RS1, the IFAC *Sustainability Framework*, the IFRS *Practice Statement* and the other discussion papers. All consistently contain references to such elements as future outlook, strategic objectives, high-level operating context, stakeholder engagement, opportunities and risk assessments, governance issues and business performance indicators or metrics.

7. Framework for Integrated Reporting and the Integrated Report – Discussion Paper (South Africa)

Another key report, published prior to the IIRC discussion paper, was the *King Discussion Paper* (2011), issued by the Integrated Reporting Committee of South Africa (IRC). This paper drew upon the *King III Code of Governance Principles for South Africa* (2009), which suggested that companies should adopt IR as a fundamental shift in the way companies and directors act and organise themselves.

This report led to the introduction, in March 2010, of a comply or explain policy relating to the preparation of published integrated reports for listed companies in South Africa. The discussion paper identifies the main objective of an integrated report as *enabling stakeholders to assess the ability of an organisation to create and sustain value over the short-, medium- and long-term*. The IRC discussion paper also regarded a key purpose of IR as assessing the ability of the entity to create and sustain value without depleting the capital assets of the business: financial, human, and environmental.

Underpinning this objective is a strong appreciation that the success of organisations is inextricably linked with three interdependent sub-systems: society, the environment, and the global economy.

The discussion paper also points out that an integrated report is not simply an amalgamation of the financial statements and the sustainability report, which confirms that IR amounts to much more than TBL accounting.

The IRC (2011) discussion paper suggests several key elements to be included in an integrated report. These are as follows:

- a concise overview of the organisation's structure, including governance and its main activities;
- a description of material risks and opportunities, based on a review of financial, social, environmental, economic, and governance issues;
- a description of the strategic objectives of the business as influenced by an assessment of the external environment and internal resource constraints; and
- an account of the organisation's performance based on its strategic objectives in terms of key performance and risk indices.

The key concerns of stakeholders in the IRC discussion paper are therefore seen to include the ability of business leaders to strategically assess the opportunities, threats and key risks facing the company and to responsibly govern and manage the available resources entrusted to them in the delivery of sustainable performance.

The discussion paper also suggests that, to scrutinise the board of directors effectively, stakeholders need a much wider range of performance metrics and risk indices than previously used, and expect much greater accountability from management about how the business sets and meets its objectives.

As IR has been effectively mandatory in South Africa since 2010/2011, a summary of the findings of how reporting has changed between pre-IR in 2009 and post-IR in 2011 has been published from a detailed comparative report of 10 South African companies (ACCA, 2012b), illustrating the considerable impact that this initiative has had in

South Africa, particularly on widening the focus of the report on a wider range of stake-holders and metrics such as risk and environmental impact.

8. Implications of the Wider Adoption of Integrated Reporting for Accounting Education

Essentially, for accounting curricula to properly align with the stated principles of IR, they must assess candidates' knowledge and understanding of the business more holistically. The main implication for professional accounting educators is an explicit signal that the accounting curriculum must draw from a broader range of business disciplines than included currently. It must incorporate more affective as well as technical competences, including ethics and professional values, and become more integrated or connected in its approach to learning and assessment.

Traditionally, the accounting curriculum has been focused mainly on the transactional rather than on the tactical or strategic levels of the business because the focus of the traditional report has been mostly about recognising, measuring and valuing assets, liabilities, income and expenditure. Because of this it has tended to concentrate more on shorter-term financial performance metrics through its focus on the periodic recording, processing, summarising and reporting of financial information for shareholders. IR, however, takes a longer-term and more sustainable view of the business and its ability to affect and be affected by its environment. As the literature reviewed in this paper demonstrates, an IR perspective requires a greater synthesis of both quantitative and qualitative information to provide a richer picture of the organisation's position, performance and prospects.

It is clear that, over many years of curriculum development in professional accounting provision, the traditional accounting curriculum, which revolved around the 'stewardship' or 'fiduciary' function of accounting as a process of *retrospection* or *review* for the shareholder, has gradually widened. Increasingly, the accounting curricula for many institutions include more content around *prospective* decision-making or decision-support functions, applicable for a much wider range of internal, external and connected stakeholders. A number of accounting curricula were mainly aimed at accountants in practice rather than at the corporate sector, or the financial services industry. Understandably, such curricula placed greater emphasis on the financial accounting and reporting functions and less emphasis on the more strategic and sustainable performance and business management functions of the organisation. There was also more focus on external audit rather than on developing proactive systems of governance, internal control or risk management. These curricula focused more on compliance and meeting rules-based legal and regulatory requirements than on principle-based approaches to financial reporting, or behaving in accordance with professional or corporate codes of ethics.

IR, and the principles behind it, therefore suggests to qualification developers that a modern accounting curriculum must include learning outcomes that relate to the key suggested elements of an integrated report as proposed consistently in the various discussion papers and frameworks highlighted in this paper, particularly within the King IRC discussion paper, the GRI, IFAC and the IIRC Frameworks.

Following from the above review and analysis of the key contributions to the debate on IR, it is possible to synthesise the recommendations and guidance issued to date to prepare a defined set of high-level outcomes that could form the high-level structure for a twenty-first-century accounting curriculum. However, two components contained within the IIRC framework (future outlook and strategic objectives) are combined under one heading in the list below, as they can be considered to be synonymous. An additional component, separately identified in the King (IRC) Discussion Paper, is the need for a review of the alignment of directors' remuneration to the performance of a company. In the other frameworks, this heading is subsumed under the governance element, but in the current economic and political climate, where such issues are of such prominence and of much greater public interest, it is recommended that this is included as a separate heading.

The outcomes of IR as a basis for an accounting curriculum, and for a twenty-first-century financial reporting model, can therefore be summarised as follows.

(a) Review the organisation, its governance structure, its core activities and business model, and how it creates and adds value for stakeholders.
(b) Assess risks and opportunities, as identified from an evaluation of financial, social, environmental, economic and governance issues.
(c) Identify and evaluate an entity's strategic objectives as informed by (a) and (b) above, taking into account sustainability issues.
(d) Evaluate the organisation's core competences to achieve these objectives sustainably in (c) above, and justify how achievement of these objectives is monitored and controlled, using short-, medium- and longer-term key performance indicators.
(e) Account for the sustainable performance of the organisation, using financial and non-financial key performance measures of its material social, environmental, economic, and financial impacts on key stakeholders.
(f) Explain the alignment of remuneration policy relating to senior executives and evaluate their performance in relation to (e) above.

The potential impact of mainstream business entities widely adopting the principles of IR are significant, for both professional and university education, and for the accounting curriculum.

Such developments should encourage curriculum developers to consider the overall structure, design and approach to delivering and assessing accounting as a discipline. It is important for the business and accounting employment sector that professional accounting bodies and university accounting departments re-design their curricula consistently with each other, to prepare modern accountants for their new challenges, regardless of where they have obtained their higher education. This is particularly important when IR and sustainability principles become mainstream reporting models rather than abstract or aspirational academic concepts.

The main changes that the above accounting reforms will require are a review of the prominence given to the overall number of subjects that need or should be taught within a programme, or whether, under IR principles, greater synthesis of certain previously discretely taught accounting disciplines could be achieved. For example, it might be sensible to combine principles of performance management with elements of strategy, risk, governance and finance, including selected material on internal audit and control principles. More qualitative reporting and assessment of entities could be introduced, based on 'substance over form' rather than the current transactional emphasis on detailed accruals-based financial adjustments.

A greater focus on more holistic value-based financial reporting models may be required, such as economic value added (EVA)$^{©}$ (Stewart, 1991), Shareholder Value Added (Rappaport, 1986) and free cash flow accounting (FCF) as underpinned by fundamental economic and risk-based models such as portfolio theory and the capital asset pricing model (CAPM).

As far as the content of curricula is concerned, more emphasis on business strategy, governance and agency will be required so that accountants develop a greater sense of corporate social responsibility and ethics, and become more aware of their obligations to stakeholders and the wider public interest.

The balance of emphasis on external financial reporting in the narrower sense may well diminish in the future and in its place a more holistic approach to reporting, based on internal management accounting information and performance management and finance based metrics and measurements, could emerge. Therefore, in the future, it is likely that there may be fewer modules called financial reporting and more with general titles such as 'corporate reporting' or even 'integrated reporting', in which the syllabuses focus much more on the qualitative and the prospective aspect of external reporting than on presenting detailed historical data.

The accounting curriculum will also need to contain more emphasis on performance and financial management at all levels of the organisation and on the link between performance management, strategy and external reporting.

Corporate reports will include more information on business outlook and strategy by presenting long-term plans and even broad budgetary information (taking into account information sensitivity analysis). The new emphasis in such reports will mean that syllabuses will need to include analysis of high-level variance and exceptions analysis in financial and performance management terms. This will be necessary to hold directors more accountable for discrepancies between actual performance and impacts, compared with forecasts already published, and to recommend performance improvements in the future.

Assessment strategies will need to adapt to meet IR's needs in the accounting curriculum at universities and within professional accounting qualifications. As formerly distinct subject areas are increasingly delivered in a more holistic and integrated way, the style and character of assessment will need to become more case-based and scenario driven. For example, final-level assessments may become fewer in number, more integrative and cross-functional in nature. Such assessments will be more of the open-book, pre-released information mode than the traditional closed-book, unseen examination.

Learners will therefore need to demonstrate higher-level synthesis and evaluation skills. They will need to analyse more unstructured information, financial, quantitative and qualitative, from a greater variety of sources, to present a more rounded evaluation of the position, performance and impacts of an entity. The focus of such assessments under the IR model of reporting will tend to become more strategic and tactical rather than transactional. Learners will therefore need to become more adept at business rather than purely financial analysis. They will need to appreciate the value of using information for its predictive capability, for prospective evaluation and for its remedial and corrective purposes, rather than from the more passive stewardship perspective.

9. How ACCA Embeds Principles of Sustainability and Integrated Reporting in the Professional Qualification Curriculum

The ACCA Qualification has been designed to meet its key stakeholders' needs and the structure of the qualification reflects the needs of employers, regulators, learning providers, ACCA members and students.

The Qualification was re-structured in December 2007 and updated in June 2011 on the basis of a major consultation and from the analysis of competency surveys and their findings. The competency surveys asked the key stakeholders what they considered to be the most important capabilities and competences of professional accountants. The ACCA curriculum and syllabuses were developed on the basis of these findings. The key stakeholder groups ACCA uses in the regular evaluation of competency needs in the profession include: a range of key employers, ACCA members, regulatory and advisory bodies, such as IFAC; professional oversight boards, such as the UK Professional Oversight Team (POT); and national educational or occupational frameworks, professional codes and standards developed for the accounting profession. Surveys of such groups and organisations, supported by the opinions of selected focus and visioning groups made up of key individuals in business, practice and learning, also contributed to the development process. Such stakeholders are regularly surveyed and it is proposed that ACCA will survey these groups explicitly on recent integrated reporting proposals and on how the ACCA Qualification structure, content and assessment will need to adapt.

In addition, ACCA has developed a competency framework for the qualification based on employer research carried out by a team of consultants. The initial findings of this research conclude that nine of the 10 main headings closely match those competences that are most prominent within the integrated reporting framework.

These include:

- corporate reporting;
- leadership and management;
- strategy and innovation;
- financial management;
- sustainable management accounting;
- audit and assurance;
- governance, risk and control;
- stakeholder relationship management; and
- professionalism and ethics.

Underpinning these headings, the range of subjects currently included in the ACCA Professional Qualification, as influenced by stakeholders in their feedback, also tend to reflect the principles of IR fairly closely.

Figure 2 shows the ACCA qualification structure as at January 2012.

10. How Integrated Reporting and Sustainability is Embedded within the ACCA Qualification

Using the main outcomes as summarised from the key discussion papers and frameworks discussed in this paper, it can be seen that ACCA's curriculum aligns quite closely with the key IR principles in its structure and coverage.

Within the Diploma in Accounting and Business level, ACCA introduces a gateway examination called 'Accountant in Business', which sets accounting in the wider business context, introducing the student to the business, how it is structured and interacts with its environment, covering stakeholder relationships, the role of corporate governance and of the accountant within business as communicator, manager and leader. This paper clearly spells out that the accountant is the link between many aspects of the business at all levels. Diploma holders also have to complete a 'Foundations in Professionalism' module, which introduces students to such concepts as fundamental principles of ethical behaviour and the duties and responsibility of accountants.

Elsewhere at the Diploma level and at the Advanced Diploma level, there is a strong emphasis on examining performance and financial management, including references to sustainability in such papers as F5, *Performance Management*, F7, *Financial Reporting*, and the assessment and management of risk in F9, *Financial Management* and within

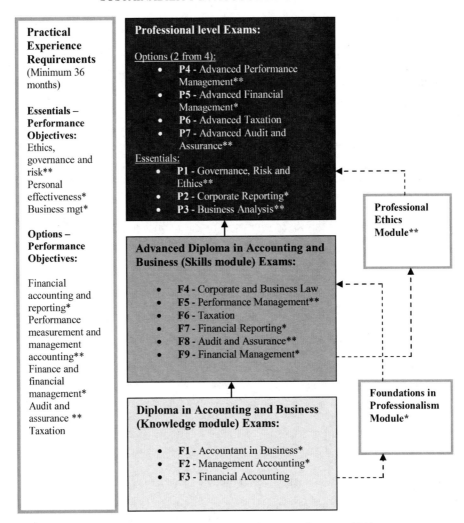

Figure 2. ACCA Professional Qualification Structure 2012.
*These subjects contain some outcomes that relate to the principles of IR and sustainability issues.
**These subjects include a substantial number of outcomes which underpin principles of IR and sustainability issues.

the F8, *Audit and Assurance* examination. These papers focus upon both qualitative and quantitative information.

ACCA has a Professional Level examination, P1, *Governance, Risk and Ethics*, which is heavily focused on key principles of IR. The governance section of the syllabus specifically addresses directors' responsibilities relating to strategy development, audit and internal control, remuneration and risk. Identification and control of risk are included in two other sections of the syllabus. There is a whole section within the syllabus devoted to professional and corporate ethics.

ACCA students also have to successfully complete an online Professional Ethics module before they are admitted to ACCA membership.

In addition, 11 of 16 of ACCA's examination syllabuses embed ethical and sustainability principles and examiners are encouraged to introduce ethical and environmental dimensions to support technical requirements to examine candidates' values and judgement as well as their knowledge. The audit examinations also cover governance aspects related to the audit and assurance functions including risk management, internal audit and internal controls.

In other syllabuses (such as management accounting, performance management, financial management and business analysis), many outcomes underpin the key principles of IR. These relate to organisational structure and strategy covered in P3, *Business Analysis*, which examines the ability of the candidate to analyse business opportunities and threats (or risks) and evaluate strategic objectives based on internal strengths and weaknesses and resource constraints. This syllabus is about examining how a candidate assesses the position and prospects or 'outlook' of a company, as well as its past performance.

The financial management examinations in the Skills Module and at the Professional Level further examine the understanding of financial risk and the main methods of responsibly mitigating exposure to such risks. The Management Accounting and Performance Management syllabuses address and examine issues related to performance measurement, planning, control and feedback, all of which are key to effective IR.

ACCA students also have to complete practical experience requirements, which include demonstrating specific performance objectives relating to principles underlying integrated reporting. These include three mandatory Performance Objectives, PO-1, *Demonstration of the application of professional ethics, values and judgment*, PO-2, *Contribute to the effective governance of an organisation*, and PO-3, *Raise awareness of non-financial risk*. The Options performance objectives, which include specific technical competences, also include content relating to elements of integrated reporting mainly in the areas of financial performance, performance measurement, financial management and management accounting.

11. Conclusions

IR has been heavily promoted in recent years, as this paper has demonstrated, but it must be recognised that the concept is not entirely new. IR has evolved from CSR as addressed in *The Corporate Report*, published over 35 years ago, and is a natural extension of many principles of environmental or 'green' accounting, sustainability reporting and TBL accounting, all of which have come to prominence at various times over many years.

Assuming that the main IR principles identified in the more recent documents reviewed in this paper become widely adopted, there are a number of key developments that may need to take place in professional and university accounting curricula to meet these changes.

It is likely that accounting curricula will need even more of a strategic rather than operational or transactional focus. They will need to adopt a longer rather than short-term outlook; present more prospective rather than retrospective analysis; include more qualitative commentary as well as quantitative information; and report on wider business performance metrics rather than on narrower external financial reporting data or audit compliance.

Modern accounting syllabuses will also need to contain more content on business risk, integrated into a range of syllabuses, rather than located in a single discrete syllabus. This content will include both financial and non-financial risk and will be mainly aimed at the strategic and tactical rather than operational levels, although this may vary depending on the subject covered.

ACCA strongly supports the latest initiatives in IR and the objectives of the IFAC, the IIRC and the IRC Frameworks, and recognises that the quality of financial reporting can only be improved by such initiatives. It is also to be welcomed that such developments may lead to an increase in accountability and transparency in corporate reporting. ACCA's CEO (Helen Brand) is a member of the strategic steering committee of the International Integrated Reporting Committee (IIRC). ACCA supports the thinking behind, and development of, the IR initiative, and will also continue to research other models as part of its focus on the future of corporate reporting (ACCA, 2011).

Such developments and improvements in the quality and lucidity of financial reporting will also provide greater insights into the performance and progress of the business and more closely hold accountable the leaders and management of such businesses. It will also require the education and training of accountants to reflect these new principles to prepare the twenty-first-century accountant for a much more challenging role in the near future.

These developments can only be in the wider public interest of improving the relevance of information for decision-making for all stakeholders, thereby allowing greater efficiency in the allocation of financial and other resources, and in adding public value.

References

ACCA (2011) *ACCA Thinks*, news release, November. Available at http://www.accanet.org/pubs/reputation/policy/statements/pol-thinks-004.pdf

ACCA (2012a) *Annual Report 2011–12*. Available at http://www.accaglobal.com/en/discover/report-accounts/2011-2012.html

ACCA (2012b) Reporting pre- and post-King III: what's the difference? Discussion paper based on J. Solomon and W. Maroun (2012) *Integrated Reporting: The New Face of Social, Ethical and Environmental Reporting in South Africa* (London: ACCA). Available at http://www.accaglobal.co.uk/en/technical-activities/technical-library/integrated-reporting.html

Accounting Standards Board (2006a) *Reporting Statement: Operating and Financial Review*, ISBN 1-84140-755-0. Available at http://www.frc.org.uk/asb/press/pub1029.html

Accounting Standards Board (2006b) *Reporting Standard 1: Operating and Financial Review*, ISBN 1 84140 683 X. Available at http://www.frc.org.uk/images/uploaded/documents/Web%20optimized%20OFR%20REPORTING%20STANDARD.pdf

Accounting Standards Steering Committee (1975) *The Corporate Report*, discussion paper, London. Available at http://www.ion.icaew.com/ClientFiles/6f45ef7e-1eff-41ff-909e-24eeb6e9ed15//The%20Corporate%20Report2.pdf

Cooper, S. and Owen, D. (2007) Corporate social reporting and stakeholder accountability: the missing link, *Accounting, Organizations and Society*, 32, pp. 649–667.

Eccles, R. G. and Krzus, M. P. (2010) *One Report: Integrated Reporting for a Sustainable Strategy* (Hoboken, NJ: John Wiley & Sons).

Elkington, J. (2004) Enter the triple bottom line, in: A. Henriques and J. Richardson (Eds) *The Triple Bottom Line – Does it All Add Up?* (London: Earthscan).

Federation of European Accountants (2012) *Fact Sheet*, January. Available at http://www.fee.be/fileupload/upload/Integrated%20Reporting%20update%20January%202020123112012501334.pdf

Gray, R., Owen, D. and Adams, C. (1996) *Accounting and Accountability* (Hemel Hempstead: Prentice Hall International).

Gray, R. H., Dey, C. R., Owen, D., Evans, R. and Zadek, S. (1997) Struggling with the praxis of social accounting: stakeholders, accountability, audits and procedures, *Accounting Auditing and Accountability Journal*, 10(3), pp. 325–364 (Hemel Hempstead: Prentice Hall International).

GRI (2006) *G3 – The Sustainability Reporting Framework*.

IAASB (2011) *The Evolving Nature of Financial Reporting; Disclosure and its Audit Implications*, IFAC.

IASB (2010a) *Conceptual Framework for Financial Reporting* (the IFRS Framework), IFAC.

IASB (2010b) *Management Commentary: A Framework for Presentation*, IFAC.

IFAC (2010) *Competent and Versatile: How Professional Accountants in Business Drive Sustainable Organizational Success*, ISBN 978-1-60815-071-7 (New York: IFAC).

IFAC (2011) *Sustainability Framework 2*, ISBN 978-1-60815-048-9 (New York: IFAC).

Integrated Reporting Committee (IRC) of South Africa (2011) *Framework for Integrated Reporting and the Integrated Report*, SAICA.

International Integrated Reporting Council (2013) *Consultation Draft of the International (IR) Framework.* Available at http://www.theiirc.org/wp-content/uploads/Consultation-Draft/Consultation-Draft-of-the-InternationalIRFramework.pdf

Mendelow, A. (1991) *Stakeholder Mapping*, Proceedings of the 2nd International Conference on Information Systems, Cambridge, MA.

Mitchell, R. K., Agle, B. R. and Wood, D. J. (1997) Toward a theory of stakeholder identification and salience: defining the principle of who and what really counts, *Academy of Management Review*, 22(4), pp. 853–888.

Owen, D., Gray, R. and Bebbington, J. (1997) Green accounting: cosmetic irrelevance or radical agenda for change? *Asia Pacific Journal of Accounting*, 4(2), pp. 175–198.

Rappaport, A. (1986) *Creating Shareholder Value: The New Standard for Business Performance* (New York: Free Press).

Smith, A. (1776/1937) *The Wealth of Nations*, E. Cannan (Ed.) (New York: Modern Library).

Stewart, G. B., III (1991) *The Quest for Value – The EVA Management Guide* (New York: Harper Collins).

Unerman, J., Bebbington, J. and O'Dwyer, B. (Eds) (2007) *Sustainability Accounting and Accountability* (Abingdon: Routledge).

University in Rotterdam in 2006. This course contained five dedicated CSR modules on awareness, strategy, embedding, reporting, and assurance and is still running, but in a modified format. Prior to this I was involved in the development of a postgraduate course in environmental auditing at the University of Amsterdam. It was intended that material from this course would be integrated into the mainstream accounting programme, but this was not achieved due to claims that the programme was already overcrowded.

Sustainability was considered marginal to businesses and perceived negatively in that it restricted businesses doing business. Sustainability is now a mainstream business concern that is directly impacting financial performance, and businesses are revising their strategies and information management accordingly. Cash flows of the past are no guarantee of those in the future. Global challenges such as climate change, resource depletion, an aging and growing population, and emerging economies require businesses to undergo major transformations in order to sustain value creation in the short, medium and long term. For example, resource depletion requires moving from a linear economy to a circular economy, with much greater emphasis on re-use and recycling. Organisations no longer have the choice to ignore these global challenges and the impacts of resource depletion/ climate change are financially visible to all. However, leading organisations recognise business opportunities in eco-products, eco-services and the value of sustainable and responsible corporate practices.

Integrated reporting requires changes across all dimensions of organisational thinking, and the embedding of this new thinking throughout the organisation. This requires changes in accounting, particularly accounting information for strategic decision-making, investment decisions, and performance improvement. Integrating reporting challenges the purpose of financial reporting and appears to support a shift away from traditional financial accountability towards driving change in organisations and wider society.

It is important to recognise that integrated reporting is not new. In the 1970s many proposed a more holistic approach to accounting incorporating economic, social and environmental aspects in annual reports (Estes, 1976; Shreuder, 1981; Bindenga, 1982). Others successfully experimented with alternative environmental and social reports (e.g. BSO/ Origin, 1991; Gray, 1997). However, these initiatives were not systematically adopted, with many different obstacles being placed in their path, including the training and education of accountants. I believe that, if accountants are to fulfil their future roles as transformative professionals, then education must play a fundamental role and Integrated Reporting in its widest sense must become part of the accounting curriculum. Leading organisations already recognise the need for accountants to work with social and environmental experts to create sustainable governance, reporting and assurance. A multidisciplinary approach towards accounting education is therefore essential, and I think this could be further emphasised in the paper.

Whilst recognising the importance of the ACCA's curriculum developments, I feel the paper underplays other developments in other accounting curricula. The paper could be criticised for its focus on a UK perspective and I would like to draw attention to major reforms towards more holistic approaches to business in continental Europe and how the European Commission and the European Federation of Accountants are responding. ACCA has students all over the world and it would be good to provide a wider view on such developments across different continents. (For example, IFAC's education guidelines on where sustainability should be addressed and the European professional accounting bodies' 'Common Content' project.) I would also draw attention to UNCTAD-ISAR's work, which examines the changes needed to accounting education, legal and governance frameworks, and the institutional role of accountancy bodies if organisations are to produce high-quality sustainable reporting.

The accounting curriculum is dominated by the role of the external accountant, despite almost half of professional accountants working in businesses. It is encouraging that this paper addresses a fuller range of the functions of accountants in organisations and bridges the gap between internal and external accounting. The connection between management and external accounting becomes critical in Integrated Reporting. Central to an integrated report is strategic management information as well as greater transparency on the organisation's business model, its management and operations. Currently accountants are not sufficiently qualified to prepare these reports, and the paper addresses how this educational gap can be filled.

Finally, I welcome the return of ethics as the foundation of accounting and accounting education. Ethics is the root from which all accounting should grow from. As a profession I believe we moved too quickly away from ethics to focus on the financial and technical aspects of accounting. It is good to step back, reflect and learn from this experience. We need to engage in a searching and critical discussion on the contemporary relevance of our profession and how accounting can create and sustain value in the long term.

References

Bindenga, A. J. (1982) Maatschappelijke verslaggeving in opmars? [Reporting to society, a new emerging trend?], *De Accountant*, 8(April), pp. 482–486.

BSO/Origin (1991) *BSO/Origin Environmental Accounts*. Available at http://www.st-andrews.ac.uk/media/csear/app2practice-docs/CSEAR_bso-1991.pdf.

Estes, R. (1976) *Corporate Social Accounting* (New York: Wiley).

Gray, R. (1997) The silent practice of social accounting and corporate social reporting in companies, in: S. Zadek, P. Prusen and R. Evans (Eds) *Building Corporate Accountability: Emerging Practices in Social and Ethical Accounting, Auditing and Reporting*, pp. 201–217 (London: Earthscan).

Owen, G. (2013) Integrated reporting – a review of developments and implications for the accounting curriculum, *Accounting Education: An International Journal*, 22(4), pp. 340–356.

Schreuder, H. (1981) *Maatschappelijke verantwoordelijkheid en maatschappelijke berichtgeving van ondernemingen* [*Social Responsibility and Reporting to Society by Corporation*] (Leiden: Stenfert Kroese).

Owen (2013) argues that these new competences require accounting to draw from a wider range of business disciplines and develop subjects that integrate performance management with strategy, risk, governance, finance, audit, and external reporting. There is a need to focus on qualitative, prospective, and holistic value-based financial reporting models. More affective (ethics and values) as well as technical competences are required, and accounting education should develop higher-level synthesis and evaluation skills, focusing on strategic and tactical aspects rather than passive financial stewardship. There should be a shift to skills in analysing business information for evaluating future prospects and reme-dial or corrective purposes. A more integrative and cross-functional approach to assess-ment is suggested (e.g. case-based and scenario-driven assessment).

All of these changes are critical to equip accountants with the knowledge, skills, and com-petences to produce Integrated Reports. However, I would like to take a more critical stance and question the ability of the profession to serve the public interest if sustainability issues are not understood or embedded in the accounting curriculum at a time when accounting's social legitimacy has been badly damaged by so many incidents and scandals. The challenge for accounting educators is to design and deliver programmes that reflect leading edge sus-tainability theories and practices as well as critically examining the role of different theories and accounting practices that contributed to society's unsustainability. Owen concentrates on the design and delivery of accounting programmes that represent many of the important aspects of integrated reporting, but two significant questions remain. These are:

1. What is the relationship between integrated reporting and sustainability?
2. Does integrated reporting provide a proper base to enable accountants to contribute to solving society's unsustainability?

Reflecting on the content and rhetoric of IIRC discussions, I believe there is a discourse that privileges shareholder value, investors, and managing risks at the expense of sustainability, stakeholder dialogue, and engagement. In my opinion, integrated reporting does not incor-porate sufficient aspects of sustainability to substantively change the world. A priori, the direct translation of the premises and principles of integrated reporting into the curriculum do not offer sufficient opportunities to advance sustainability. Moreover, the taken-for-granted considerations behind the current discussion paper point to a economic rationale – dominated by financial performance and risk management – which must be challenged to transform this hidden curriculum into more transformative educational experiences, enabling accountants to act in the public interest in a highly globalised and economically endangered context. Accountants are not just technicians practising a technical craft, but are part of broader processes of reality construction (Carter, 2011); a reality that demands much more sustainability than suggested by integrated reporting.

Education involves the acquisition of technical knowledge but is also critical to how people understand the world (Thomson and Bebbington, 2005). Accountants need to under-stand the world and businesses from a sustainability perspective and, currently, integrated reporting does not allow this. Integrated reporting can and should be re-constructed more sustainably, and this would form a base for 'accounting FOR sustainability' education.

Adapting the accounting curriculum to integrated reporting is difficult, but feasible. It involves displacing silo thinking, stewardship of financial capital, a historic orientation, short-termism, narrow scope of disclosures, compliance orientation, and outmoded com-munication media. Integrated reporting requires integrated and holistic thinking, multi-dimensional stewardship, future orientation, strategic information, longer time-frames, wider disclosures, transparency, principles orientation, and new media (e.g. XBRL tech-nology-enabled reports; see FEE, 2011a, 2011b, 2012; AECA, 2012). If we seek to serve the public interest, the accounting profession must aspire to influence businesses (in a sustainable direction) and accountants' learning experience should incorporate an authentic understanding of stakeholder engagement, materiality, boundary-setting, and multidisciplinary team-working. However, these challenges are significant, and I concur with Saravanamuthu and Filling (2004) that accountants, in their souls, have never accepted the full implications of being public accountants. To be public accountants requires understanding sustainability, challenging the current manifestation of integrated reporting, and designing new accounting practices that do change the mindset, culture, or behaviour of managers, policy-makers, and society to induce the social changes.

I am not suggesting that embedding integrated reporting in the accounting curriculum is futile. On the contrary, I am appealing to an openness to learn from the past, the development of other integrated, sustainability reporting practices and their corresponding criticisms. It would appear that some of these lessons have been ignored, as evidenced by the narrow scope of the integrated reporting discussion paper. Indeed, FEE (2011a) underscores the importance of reflecting on the interconnections between environmental, social, governance, and financial factors in decision-making, making clear the link between sustainability and economic value, and of providing the necessary framework to systematically account for environmental and social factors. GRI also suggests that stakeholder engagement is under-developed in integrated reporting and that this is a problem in developing effective sustainability reports. The integrated report does not explicitly recognise accounting as 'a form of social power' (Boyce, 2000, p. 27) or stress the role of accounting in developing accountability, promoting transparent decision-making, creating environmental and social visibilities, or exposing the standpoints of interested parties (Brown, 2009). These are critical issues for future accounting curriculum development if the accounting profession is to effectively serve the public interest and lead to a more sustainable world.

References

AECA (2012) *Información Integrada: El Cuadro Integrado de Indicadores (CII-FESG) y su Taxonomía XBRL* (Asociación Española de Contabilidad y Administración de Empresas).

Boyce, G. (2000) Public discourse and decision making: exploring possibilities for financial, social and environmental accounting, *Accounting, Auditing & Accountability Journal*, 13(1), pp. 27–64.

Brown, J. (2009) Democracy, sustainability and dialogic accounting technologies: taking pluralism seriously, *Critical Perspectives on Accounting*, 20(3), pp. 313–342.

Carter, D. (2011) Accountant's truth: knowledge and ethics in the financial world, *European Accounting Review*, 20(3), pp. 583–594.

FEE (2011a) *Fact Sheet on Integrated Reporting* (Fédération des Experts comptables Européens).

FEE (2011b) *Response to IIRC Discussion Paper 'Towards Integrated Reporting' – Communicating Value in the 21st Century* (Fédération des Experts comptables Européens).

FEE (2012) *Fact Sheet on Integrated Reporting, update* (Fédération des Experts comptables Européens).

Owen, G. (2013) Integrated reporting – a review of developments and their implications for the accounting curriculum, *Accounting Education: An International Journal*, 22(4), pp. 340–356.

Saravanamuthu, K. and Filling, S. (2004) A critical response to managerialism in the academy, *Critical Perspectives on Accounting*, 15(4–5), pp. 437–452.

Thomson, I. and Bebbington, J. (2005) Social and environmental reporting in the UK: a pedagogic evaluation, *Critical Perspectives on Accounting*, 16(5), pp. 507–533.

Arguably, the above comment may simply represent a potential difference in how integrated reporting and sustainability are understood as related concepts underlying accounting curriculum development. My paper was written on the assumption that stances on agency have evolved from viewing corporate responsibility from discrete, linear positions situated along a political continuum (Gray, Owen and Adams, 1996) to one where integrated reporting as a concept is based on the accountant's role as agent of a much broader constituency of principals, which *ipso facto* must adopt a more holistic view of the business and how it interacts with the wider world. Integrated reporting, as discussed in the paper, would therefore regard environmental sustainability as only one (albeit very important) lens of a more multi-dimensional and integrated view of the business, which includes political, economic, social, technological, environmental and legal (ethical) considerations.

Specifically in response to the above quotation, it is agreed that accounting education should involve more than acquiring technical knowledge, and my paper makes it clear that developing affective competencies and soft skills are increasingly important to accountants and how they should interact with others, both within and outside their organization, and indeed in how they understand the world and their responsibilities within it.

The paper therefore argues that, as presented and described, integrated reporting principles would not only allow but would actively promote a better understanding of the world and how the organization and its behaviour impacts upon it, from a broader and longer-term perspective than is the case currently.

Referring back to the main elements of an integrated report,

- having a future outlook and a strategic and organizational overview of the business model within an operating context; and
- having an awareness and a knowledge and understanding of risks and opportunities facing the business

are crucial to integrated reporting principles and, arguably, to having a sustainable view of the world.

In addition, building leadership capabilities, embedding a risk culture, introducing governance structures and designing performance management systems, properly underpinned by sustainability principles, are developments entirely consistent with integrated reporting principles.

In summary, the main argument put forward in my paper asserts that the main elements underpinning the proposed integrated reporting models will, by implication, support the concept of sustainability through accountants gaining a better understanding of the relationship between the business and the wider world, and how they impact upon and interact with each other. The paper suggests that curriculum development based on integrated reporting principles should lead accountants to better recognize their responsibility to the business and the public interest. Such developments should lead to accountants being better *trusted* to appropriately measure, assess, evaluate, and report these impacts and to make and support more sustainable and responsible decisions.

Kamp-Roelands (2013) also welcomed the paper and what it says about curriculum changes in accounting education, to encourage the 'mindshift' needed to enable accountants to support business, government, and other organizations to move towards a more sustainable future. In addition, she finds it encouraging that the paper addresses the wider range of functions of accountants and the need to bridge the gap between financial reporting and management accounting, which is critical to a more holistic view of business and to integrated reporting generally.

Kamp-Roelands (2013) points out that climate change, resource depletion, changing demographics and emerging economies all represent global challenges that require businesses to undergo major transformations in order to sustain value creation in the short-, medium- and long-term. It is argued that integrated reporting requires changes across all dimensions of organizational thinking and embedding this new thinking throughout the organization. Many of the arguments used within the paper concur and support this view.

However, Kamp-Roelands (2013) does criticize the paper for its UK focus and claims that it underplays developments in other accounting curricula, despite the fact that the ACCA has students all over the world. To refute this criticism it is necessary to point out that, while the paper initially focused on UK developments in financial reporting, which provided the platform from which integrated reporting as a concept would emerge, particularly *The Corporate Report*, the paper does then focus quite heavily on more recent international developments. For example, the paper discusses, in some detail, initiatives from the International Federation of Accountants (IFAC), the European Federation of Accountants (FEE), and features the *Framework of Integrated Reporting and the Integrated Report* from South Africa.

In summary, as a final rejoinder to these excellent Commentaries, it is to be welcomed that both commentators seem to broadly support these initiatives and the aims of the paper. However, Correa Ruiz's (2013) view that integrated reporting may not be a proper base for sustainable accounting can be challenged from the perspective that integrated reporting may in fact be more comprehensive as a financial reporting model that focuses on sustainability as part of a wider concept of corporate, social, environmental and public accountability.

In response to Kamp-Roelands' (2013) assertion that the paper may be too UK-centric, it has been explained that the paper does genuinely attempt to take a global view of integrated reporting, specifically emphasizing IFAC, GRI and South African initiatives in developing this important concept.

References

Correa Ruiz, C. (2013) A commentary on 'Integrated reporting – a review of developments and their implications for the accounting curriculum', *Accounting Education: An International Journal*, 22(4), pp. 360–362.

Gray, R., Owen, D. and Adams, C. (1996) *Accounting and Accountability: Social and Environmental Accounting in a Changing World* (Hemel Hempstead: Prentice Hall International).

Kamp-Roelands, N. (2013) A commentary on 'Integrated reporting – a review of developments and their implications for the accounting curriculum', *Accounting Education: An International Journal*, 22(4), pp. 357–359.

Owen, G. (2013) Integrated reporting – a review of developments and their implications for the accounting curriculum, *Accounting Education: An International Journal*, 22(4), pp. 340–356.

Saravanamuthu, K. and Filling, S. (2004) A critical response to managerialism in the academy, *Critical Perspectives on Accounting*, 15(4–5), pp. 437–452.

Thomson, I. and Bebbington, J. (2005) Social and environmental reporting in the UK: a pedagogic evaluation, *Critical Perspectives on Accounting*, 16(5), pp. 507–533.

long history. As noted by Brunold in 2006, 'for more than 20 years environmental edu-cation has been a national [German] and international aim as well as an accepted goal in the field of educational policy' (Brunhold, 2006, p. 222). In Australia, incorporating ecologically sustainable development principles into the curriculum of universities was an objective endorsed by the Council of Australian Governments two decades ago (Department of Sustainability, Environment, Water, Population and Communities, 1992).

Sustainability, in general, and environmental sustainability in particular, have particular relevance for accounting education. Gray (1990) has argued that accounting plays a role in the process of environmental degradation. It follows that accountants have a responsibility to 'help re-orientate business actions to the biosphere' (Bebbington *et al.*, 1994, p. 109). A number of studies discuss the issues associated with, and the extent to which sustainability is incorporated into business education (e.g. Bebbington, 1997; Gibson, 1997; Jucker, 2002; Kelly and Alam, 2009; Adams *et al.*, 2011; von der Heidt and Lamberton, 2011), and some resources are beginning to emerge for accounting academics wishing to incorporate sustain-ability into their existing courses (e.g. Fleischman and Schuele, 2006; Wynder, 2011).

Thomas argued in 2004, however, that the adoption of effective sustainability education in higher education (across all disciplines) was at a low level, and he describes some of the barriers, including a lack of culture in which value and priority are given to sustainability (Thomas, 2004). More recently, Fisher and Bonn (2011) found that more than half of Aus-tralian universities do not explicitly incorporate sustainability into their business pro-grammes, and Naeem and Neal (2011) provide similar results for the Asia Pacific region.

Furthermore, teaching sustainability, even if it changes attitudes, may be insufficient to change behaviour. For example, a study by Touche Ross Management Consultants (1990) found that UK managers were not converting concerns about the environment into positive actions. More recently, this gap between attitudes and action has been identified as preva-lent throughout society (Kollmuss and Agyemann, 2002; Zsóka, 2005). Csutora (2012, p. 146) summarises previous research and notes that the gap between pro-environmental attitudes and actual behaviour 'is due to the complex nature of reality and economic-struc-tural factors'. In other words, an organisational and/or individual commitment to sustain-ability may be insufficient to drive sustainable actions if there are conflicting incentives and pressures.

Evaluation and reward are part of the economic-structural reality in which managers make decisions that will affect their organisation's environmental impact. An important function of evaluation and reward is to communicate values and motivate desired behav-iour. Dysfunctional behaviour occurs when evaluation and rewards are not carefully linked to the organisation's values (Hopwood, 1972). Therefore, in this study we focus on the extent to which environmental measures are viewed in the same way as other important lead indicators of future financial performance.

Furthermore, this study considers the role of education and experience in creating the understanding necessary to recognise the strategic importance of lead indicators, gener-ally, and environmental performance, specifically. Testing the effect of education is timely in the 'Decade of Sustainability Education'. We also test the effect of experience: is experience necessary to understand complex systems, of which environmental perform-ance is a part? Do practising accountants view environmental performance as a strategic imperative, or do economic priorities acquired through experience take precedence?

Environmental performance, along with social and economic performance, is a pillar of sustainability. We focus, in this paper, on environmental performance because its strategic significance has been argued widely (e.g. Berry and Rondinelli, 1998; Brown, Dillard and Marshall, 2005; Cormier, Magnan and Van Velthoven, 2005). Planning instruments, including the balanced scorecard (BSC), have been identified as a means of integrating environmental performance into an organisation's strategy (Epstein and Wisner, 2001; Figge *et al.*, 2002; Moller and Schaltegger, 2005).

In a performance evaluation task using a BSC we find that experienced accounting controllers and third-year business students both recognised the importance of traditional lead indicators. Furthermore, the emphasis on lead performance indicators, including environmental performance, increased with education. Importantly, however, experienced accounting controllers placed less weight on environmental performance than did third-year business students. What is not clear is whether these graduates will be a new generation of more environmentally-conscious accountants, or if it is just rhetoric that will not stand up to the reality experienced in organisations.

2. Prior Literature and Hypothesis Development

The importance of sustainability as an objective for profit-seeking organisations, and therefore its place in a business curriculum, is not without question. The notable economist Friedman argued that if sustainability, or the related notion of Corporate Social Responsibility (CSR), does not increase shareholder value then it is an illegitimate use of an organisation's resources (Friedman, 1970). Consistent with this view is the need to develop a business case for sustainability in which investments in social and environmental performance must be linked to financial performance. This view will be discussed in further detail below.

There are, however, alternative perspectives to the profit-centric view, namely the stakeholder-accountability and critical theory approaches (Brown and Fraser, 2006). Proponents of stakeholder-accountability argue that social and environmental performance are important organisational objectives in their own right, because the organisation has a responsibility to various stakeholders in addition to shareholders (e.g. Chen, 1975; Kelly and Alam, 2009). Critical theorists go a step further in arguing that environmental measures should not be incorporated into existing accounting models because to do so leads to irredeemable contamination by the ideological assumptions underlying the existing system (Maunders and Burritt, 1991). In this view the role of a business education is to critique the capitalist paradigm (see Bebbington, 1997 for a discussion of the implication of these views for accounting education), or at least adjust it to include a recognition of the contribution of social and environmental capital (Hahn and Figge, 2011).

Despite these concerns, the dominant paradigm (according to Brown and Fraser, 2006), and the paradigm underpinning this study, is that a business case can be presented for investing in social and environmental performance (e.g. Jagersma, 2009; Lee, Faff and Langfield-Smith, 2009; Molina-Azorín *et al.*, 2009). In 2002 it was noted that:

> Responsible management of the environment and resource productivity are generally predicted to be key aspects for future competitiveness and therefore it's important to treat environmental and social criteria as being on a par with economic factors in their operative and strategic decision making. (Grablowitz, Rudeloff and Voss, 2002, p. 77)

There is some evidence that educators are beginning to incorporate CSR/sustainability into their business courses and programmes (Naeem and Neal, 2011). For example, popular management accounting textbooks in Australia (e.g. Langfield-Smith, Thorne and Hilton, 2012) now have a chapter focussed on sustainability. Furthermore, in Horngren *et al.* (2010) sustainability is integrated throughout the entire textbook. As noted in the Preface (p. xvii),

> Another important innovation in this book is a chapter dedicated to explaining the rationale and principles of sustainability, which provides the basis for considering the importance of

social and environmental issues in the various strategic and operational decisions discussed throughout this text.

A notable resource for accounting academics is Fleischman and Schuele's paper 'Green accounting: a primer' (2006). The extent to which these changes are leading to greater environmental consciousness is yet to be determined, however, and various authors have discussed the difficulty in teaching the complexity surrounding sustainability (Atwater and Pittman, 2006; MacVaugh and Norton, 2012).

The complex relationship between CSR (including environmental performance) and financial performance is also evident in empirical research (e.g. McWilliams and Siegel, 2000; Lee, Faff and Langfield-Smith, 2009; Peloza, 2009; Schreck, 2011). The general consensus of these studies is that there is a positive, or at worst neutral, relationship between investments in CSR and subsequent financial performance. As previously noted, underlying our study is the notion that CSR, including good environmental performance, can have significant economic benefit in the future. However, the relationship between environmental performance and financial performance is complex and understanding it requires education or experience.

The BSC is a mechanism by which key performance indicators can be presented in order to focus attention on critical measures and highlight relationships between leading and lagging measures. A number of authors have argued for inclusion of sustainability measures, including environmental performance, into the BSC (Epstein and Wisner, 2001; Figge et al., 2002; Alewine and Stone, 2009; Kaplan and Wisner, 2009).

An important feature of the BSC, which distinguishes it from other performance measurement systems, is its emphasis on causal relationships (Kaplan and Norton, 1996, 2000; Hoque and James, 2000; Speckbacher, Bischof and Pfeiffer, 2003). Recognising the lagged nature of financial performance, the BSC identifies the lead indicators that can be linked in a set of cause–effect relationships to future financial performance (Kaplan and Norton, 1993, 2000). It has been argued that such an approach is important in overcoming an over-reliance on current financial measures of performance (Kaplan and Norton, 1996). In a study of BSC adopters in German-speaking countries, Speckbacher, Bischof and Pfeiffer (2003) find that 'improved company results in the long term' and 'stronger consideration of non-financial drivers of performance' are two of the most important expected benefits of the BSC.

The BSC communicates the organisation's strategic priorities and critical success factors. Failure to achieve targets for measures included in the BSC is an indication that achieving the organisation's strategy is in danger. Despite this, research has found that simply including measures in the BSC does not ensure that they will be attended to in performance evaluation decisions (Banker, Chang and Pizzini, 2004; Dilla and Steinbart, 2005). Furthermore, not placing any weight on included measures creates internal conflict between the evaluator and evaluated manager (Wong-On-Wing et al., 2007).

In order for evaluators to place weight on lead indicators, they must understand and believe that the anticipated impact on financial performance will eventually accrue. Many organisations, however, do not understand the causal linkages within their BSC generally (Ittner, Larcker and Meyer, 2003), and the strategic importance of social and environmental performance specifically (Peloza, 2009). This may be because the investments in lead indicators will only lead to improved financial performance in subsequent periods. For example, in their quasi-experimental field study of actual BSC implementation in a banking institution, Davis and Albright (2004) find that financial measures increase with improving lead indicators, but not initially. Indeed, in their study the financial performance of the control group (i.e. non-BSC adopters) went up relative to the BSC adopters for the first six months. Similarly, Crabtree and DeBusk (2008) conducted a longitudinal study and found that shareholder returns were not significantly better until the second year after adoption of the BSC. The lagged nature of financial performance has important implications for managerial performance evaluation. If lead indicators are not incorporated into evaluations, myopic managers will have little incentive to make the necessary investments.

Cognitive limitations help explain the failure of evaluators to effectively use the BSC. Although the BSC is a specific attempt to focus attention on a limited number of performance measures, using it for performance evaluation is still a complex task. If taken individually, the 20–25 measures far exceed what individuals can effectively deal with in working memory. 'Thus, the volume of data in a balanced scorecard suggests that it may overload human decision makers with information' (Lipe and Salterio, 2002, p. 532).

To the extent that evaluators do not understand the strategic significance of the performance measures (Banker, Chang and Pizzini, 2004), and are unable to deal with that ambiguity (Liedtka, Church and Ray, 2008), they tend to focus on common measures of performance with which they are familiar (Lipe and Salterio, 2000; Banker, Chang and Pizzini, 2004). Hence, causal models are important in recognising the strategic significance of lead performance indicators. Causal models may be developed through education and experience (Lei, Slocum and Pitts, 1999; Rennie and Gibbins, 1993; Atwater and Pittman, 2006).

The strategic importance of some lead indicators, such as employee training and quality management, have long been advocated by academics, incorporated into university curricula, and broadly accepted by practising managers (Ishikawa, 1985; Luther, 1992; Johnson, 1994). Important in this process of acceptance has been the recognition that these strategic investments will ultimately lead to improved financial performance (Johnson, 1994; Shank and Govindarajan, 1994; Chenhall, 1997; Heskett, Sasser and Schlesinger, 1997; Samson and Terziovski, 1999). However, unless the cause–effect relationships linking lead indicators to financial performance are recognised and understood, evaluators are more likely to focus attention on financial (i.e. lagged) performance measures. Since the schemas by which cause–effect relationships are understood are developed through experience and instruction, we predict that experience and education will increase the emphasis placed on lead indicators.

H1a Experienced accounting controllers will place more weight on lead indicators in their evaluation of managerial performance than will third-year business students.

H1b Third-year business students will place more weight on lead indicators in their evaluation of managerial performance than will first-year business students.

There are various reasons why environmental performance is important to organisations. One explanation is that external constituents must be satisfied that the organisation is operating within societal values and boundaries (e.g. Cho, 2009). Consistent with this view is the increasing number of organisations that are expressing a commitment to, and reporting on, their social and environmental performance. For example, Wheeler and Elkington (2001) noted that the 1990s saw a dramatic increase in corporate environmental reporting in Europe. The reasons given include public relations and legal compliance, but also a perceived duty to the environment and maintaining competitive advantage.

In terms of internal management and reporting, it has been argued that social and environmental performance can be directly linked to financial performance (Lee, Faff and Langfield-Smith, 2009). Proponents of the so-called 'business case for sustainability/CSR' argue that measures of social and environmental performance are important determinants of future economic performance. The implication is that social and environmental performance are critical performance indicators that deserve careful managerial attention. This approach is evident in popular Australian management accounting textbooks (e.g. Horngren *et al.*, 2010). In that sense, environmental performance is another lead indicator, similar to the lead indicators considered in H1.

Despite the arguments that environmental performance is a strategic imperative, it is not clear whether experienced accounting controllers or university students understand or believe the rhetoric. Furthermore, even believing the rhetoric does not necessarily influence decision-making, particularly if the relationships are not clearly understood or other factors take precedence. Previous research (Chan and Milne, 1999; Rikhardsson and Holm, 2008) has provided conflicting experimental evidence regarding the extent to which environmental performance is factored into investment decisions. Chan and Milne (1999) found that poor environmental performance affected the long-term investment strategies of analysts and accountants, but not their short-term investments. In Rikhardsson and Holm (2008), students were able to recognise the importance of qualitative environmental performance measures for short-term investment horizons, but not quantitative measures.

Therefore, our second hypothesis is a joint test of whether participants believe that environmental performance is strategically important, and if they have sufficient understanding to incorporate environmental measures into a complex performance evaluation task. For the same reasons given in H1, we predict that both experience and education provide understanding that will increase the recognition of the strategic significance of environmental performance.

H2a Experienced accounting controllers will place more weight on environmental measures in their evaluation of managerial performance than will third-year business students.

H2b Third-year business students will place more weight on environmental measures in their evaluation of managerial performance than will first-year business students.

3. Method and Data

An experimental design was chosen to determine the emphasis placed on lead performance measures because, as noted by Rikhardsson and Holm (2008), it is more likely to determine actual decision-making behavior, which may well differ from socially acceptable attitudes captured in surveys.

3.1 *Task Description*

Participants were asked to take on the role of Financial Controller of Chemico Inc and evaluate the performance of three plant managers based on measures presented in a BSC format. Wynder (2011) describes the use of this case study to create a schema by which the importance of lead indicators, generally, and environmental performance, specifically, can be taught. In this study, however, the case is used to evaluate the individual's existing schema and so the strategy map was only provided in the debriefing.

The instrument is based on one developed by Lipe and Salterio (2000) and subsequently used in a number of other studies (Banker, Chang and Pizzini, 2004; Libby, Salterio and Webb, 2004; Kaplan and Wisner, 2009; Wong-On-Wing *et al.*, 2007). Of particular interest is the use of this approach to determine the weighting that the evaluator places on particular perspectives of the balanced scorecard. Because the only difference is the relative performance of the three managers on particular perspectives, any difference in their evaluation can be attributed to a greater or lesser weighting on those perspectives.

The targets for each manager were the same, and each plant had been established six months previously. This is significant because it means that investments in lead indicators of performance would only be starting to flow through the causal linkages toward financial performance. This applies to the lead performance indicators generally, and also to the environmental measures specifically. For example, poor performance on employee training or toxic emissions may not have financial consequences in the first six months of operations, but may flow through in time as business processes, customer satisfaction, and fines negatively impact on financial performance. The ability to anticipate the effects of the lead measures of performance will depend on the participant's schema (i.e. their understanding of the relationships between all of the performance measures).

In the scorecards used for this study (see Table 1) the performance was contrived such that, on average across all measures, the first two managers performed equally well. Manager A, however, was putting into practice the organisation's strategy of investing in employee training with resulting employee satisfaction, reduced turnover, and implementation of improvements. Productivity was beginning to show signs of improvement and customer satisfaction and retention were also beginning to show improvement over targets. However, Manager A was not yet achieving targets for market share, revenue or net profit margin. In general, it can be observed that Manager A was performing well on the lead indicators of performance and, based on the organisation's strategy, this could be expected to result in superior financial performance in the future.

In contrast, Manager B was achieving well above target in all of the financial (i.e. lag) indicators of performance, except reduction in production costs. Upon further analysis it can be seen that this is achieved at the expense of performance in factors which, according to the organisation's successful strategy, determine financial performance in the future. Specifically, the lead indicators of performance suggest that investments were not being made in employee training and the result could be seen in employee dissatisfaction and turnover. Employee suggestions are above target, but are of poor quality, as indicated by fewer improvements being implemented. Employee productivity and capacity utilisation are also high, but quality is poor and customer satisfaction and retention are below target. Market share is high, achieved by a reduction in price, without a reduction in production costs. In summary, financial performance is significantly above target, but the lead indicators of performance suggest that the organisation's strategy was not being pursued, and the superior financial performance is unlikely to be sustained into the future.

Environmental performance for Managers A and B was contrived so that it would not be a significant issue in the comparison of these two managers. Performance on environmental measures for these two managers is equivalent (the maximum individual difference is three percentage points), and close to target (maximum 10% above target). In this way differences in a participant's evaluation of Managers A and B provides the basis for testing their understanding of the importance of generally-accepted lead indicators. The importance placed on poor environmental performance was measured by differences in the evaluation of Manager C between groups.

Manager C's performance was positive on all four of the BSC perspectives commonly used. Although not quite achieving the target for employee training, the other measures (i.e. satisfaction, turnover, suggestions, and improvements) are all above target. Manager C is also performing well on financial performance measures. The important feature of Manager C's performance is that environmental performance is significantly below targets (in total, 70% worse than targets). Note the toxic air and water emissions, and the accidental release of untreated waste. Performance for Manager C was contrived

to indicate very poor environmental performance on measures that carry significant risk. Poor environmental performance can affect reputation, create liabilities, and can increase government regulation that will decrease financial performance in the future (Horngren *et al.*, 2010). In addition to these potential impacts, toxic emissions raise ethical issues that are of immediate concern.

The scorecards were designed based on the causal links implicit in the company's strategy, which was provided to participants. Note that environmental performance is not explicitly included in the strategy. Furthermore, although third-year students had studied the importance of sustainability, they had not previously seen sustainability measures within the context of a BSC and attention was not drawn to the environmental measures when presenting the task to the participants. In this way every attempt was made to avoid a demand effect so that the weighting that individuals placed on the environmental measures would provide a true indication of the importance that they attributed to environmental performance.

Specifically, all participants were provided with the following:

> Chemico Inc. has a very successful strategy focussed on careful management of the costs of production through continually reducing production costs and the effective utilisation of their expensive plant and equipment. Chemico Inc. seeks to capture market share by providing the cheapest product on the market; however, quality is also important.

> The production process involves thousands of variables that must be monitored and adjusted to determine the energy requirements and yield (output compared with input). Furthermore, the highly toxic waste must undergo expensive treatment before being released. Highly trained and experienced engineers are the key to ensuring that the process is efficient and that improvements are continually identified.

> In summary, Chemico's strategy is to invest in training and workplace conditions to improve the engineers' innovation and process management skills. This then results in more efficient operations and lower production costs. Market share then increases through low prices while maintaining a high gross margin.

> The production process requires **huge amounts of energy** which has lead Chemico Inc. to recently set up three new plants in China where there is an abundance of **low cost coal**. The plants were **established 6 months ago** and it is now time to evaluate their performance. (emphasis as in original).

3.2 *Participants*

The participants comprised individuals from three groups. The first were experienced accounting controllers attending a professional conference in Germany. 31 controllers

Table 2. Descriptive statistics and dependent variables: mean (std. dev.).

	Students		
	1st-year students (*n* = 55)	3rd-year students (*n* = 32)	Controllers (*n* = 26)
Work experience at managerial level	0.3300	0.2400	8.880 (7.941)
Gender	73.9% female	56% female	36.8% female
Evaluation Manager A (good lead indicators)	5.409 (1.7243)	6.625 (1.9838)	6.7308 (2.0309)
Evaluation Manager B (poor lead indicators)	6.727 (2.0134)	6.094 (1.9404)	5.885 (2.6280)
Evaluation Manager C (poor environmental performance)	7.136 (2.0445)	6.547 (1.9690)	8.231 (2.103)

completed the task, 26 of whom had at least two years' experience and so were included in the study. The level of experience at managerial level for this group ranged from 2 to 36 years (mean = 8.8 years, standard deviation = 7.9 years). Evaluating performance is an important function of the accounting controller. Furthermore, discussion of the BSC (although not including social or environmental performance) was included in the conference. It can also be noted that these controllers all had university education, although the content of that university education is likely to differ significantly and be overshadowed by their practical experience.

The second group comprised first-year business students from the Baden-Württemberg Cooperative State University, Ravensburg, Germany (27 students) and the University of the Sunshine Coast, Australia (28 students). Students with more than two years of work experience were excluded.

The third group comprised third-year business students from the Baden-Württemberg Cooperative State University, Ravensburg, Germany (11 students) and the University of the Sunshine Coast, Australia (21 students). Again, students with more than two years of work experience were excluded. The BSC and sustainability are taught at both institutions.

Inclusion of Australian and German students raises the potential for cultural differences that might influence the emphasis placed on lead indicators, generally, and environmental measures, specifically. Although such cultural analysis is beyond the scope of this paper, it warrants a brief discussion here.

The two countries from which participants were recruited, Australia and Germany, have very similar and relatively high scores (82.5 and 82.8) for social and institutional capacity for environmental sustainability, according to the Environmental Sustainability Index developed by the Global Leaders of Tomorrow Environment Task Force of the World Economic Forum (2001). Social and institutional capacity is a composite measure which refers to 'the extent that [a country] has in place institutions and underlying social patterns of skills, attitudes, networks that foster effective responses to environmental challenges' (Global Leaders, 2001, p. 9). This measure also includes the private sector's responsiveness to environmental problems (Husted, 2005). On this basis we do not expect a difference between the students from Australia and those from Germany, and we believe that the experienced controllers are representative of experienced management accountants in Australia, although further research would be necessary to confirm this. Post hoc tests (Scheffe and Bonferroni) revealed no significant differences between Australian first-year students and German first-year students, or Australian third-year students and German third-year students, for any of the dependent variables. The implications of cultural differences are further considered, however, in the conclusions section of this paper.

3.3 Dependent Variables

Participants were asked to evaluate each manager on a 13-point scale with seven anchors, ranging from 'Reassign: sufficient improvement unlikely (0)' to 'Excellent: far beyond expectations, manager excels (12)'.

As noted, overall Managers A and B performed equally well with a virtually identical total percentage above target. Manager A performed better, however, on the lead measures of performance (primarily learning and growth and internal processes), and Manager B performed poorly on the lead indicators but well on lag indicators of performance (financial). Manager C performed much better on the four traditional BSC measures. Very poor performance (70% below target) on the environmental measures, however, meant that net performance across all measures was slightly lower (32% versus 35% for A and B). There-fore, the evaluation of Manager A indicates the weighting placed on positive lead indi-cators, the evaluation of Manager B indicates the weighting placed on negative lead indicators, and the evaluation of Manager C indicates the weighting placed on poor environmental performance.

4. Results

The hypotheses were tested based on planned contrasts. In order to determine the effect of experience on the emphasis placed on lead performance measures (H1a), third-year uni-versity students were compared to experienced controllers. Hypothesis H1a is not sup-ported: there were no significant differences between third-year university students and experienced accounting controllers in the evaluations of Manager A (good lead indicators) or Manager B (poor lead indicators).

H1b considered the effect of education. Third-year students (from H1a) were compared with first-year students. Hypothesis H1b is supported: third-year students gave higher evaluations of Manager A (6.625 versus 5.409) and this difference is significant ($t = 28.907$, $p = 0.000$ one-tailed). Also consistent with the hypothesis, third-year students gave a lower evaluation of Manager B (with poor lead indicators) (6.094 versus 6.727) ($t = 26.826$, $p = 0.000$ one-tailed).

Together, the results of H1 suggest that an understanding of the importance of lead indi-cators, generally, was acquired through university education. Furthermore, that the under-standing acquired through education was sufficient to incorporate lead indicators into the performance evaluation.

Hypothesis H2 focused on environmental performance as a specific lead performance indicator. Manager C performed well on traditional measures found in the BSC, but very poorly on environmental performance. Therefore, a lower evaluation recognises the strategic significance of the poor environmental performance. In hypothesis H2a experienced accounting controllers were compared to third-year university students. We found a significant difference. Contrary to our hypothesis, however, we found that students penalised the poor environmental performance more than did the controllers (6.547 versus 8.231). This difference is significant ($t = 3.131$, $p = 0.002$ two-tailed). Therefore, H2a is not supported: experience did not increase the weighting placed on environmental performance.

Hypothesis H2b predicted that university education would increase the weighting placed on environmental performance. Third-year students were compared with first-year students. Hypothesis H2b is supported: third-year students gave a lower evalu-ation for Manager C (6.547 versus 7.136), and this difference is significant ($t = 30.210$, $p = 0.000$ one-tailed).

4.1 *Further Analysis*

An assumption that we made in this study was that participants, through experience and education, would develop a causal model by which environmental performance would be recognised as a lead indicator. An alternative explanation is that environmental measures are perceived as being important, regardless of any potential financial impact. This is consistent with the stakeholder-accountability perspective, recognising the respon-sibility that the company has beyond shareholders to external stakeholders.

In further analysis we explored the correlation between evaluations of Manager B (poor lead indicators) and Manager C (poor environmental performance). If educated and experienced participants viewed environmental performance in the same way as other lead indicators, we would expect to see a significant positive correlation between their evaluations of these two managers. The correlations, however, were negative and insignificant for both experienced controllers and third-year students. The consequences of this are explored in the next section.

5. Conclusions and Further Research

Many organisations espouse a commitment to the environment and various studies have described the extent and motivations for environmental disclosure (e.g. Cormier, Magnan and Van Velthoven, 2005). The emphasis has been on the relationship between the organisation and external stakeholders, and concern has been raised that external environmental reporting is merely window-dressing. The true test of an organisation's commitment to the environment lies in the internal measures of performance that drive managerial decision-making.

It is not enough, however, to include environmental measures in the BSC. Managers may still see such measures as being irrelevant if they are ignored by their evaluator. Evaluators may ignore these measures if they do not understand or believe that environmental performance is strategically important. In this study we have measured recognition of the strategic importance of environmental performance, not through an attitude survey, which would suffer from an acceptability bias, but through a task in which the participants evaluate managerial performance. The necessary trade-offs and the complicated nature of the evaluation more closely mirror the real world and provide a truer indication of the value that these individuals actually place on environmental performance.

Recall that H1 found that education increased the weighting on traditional lead indicators. Education also increased the weighting on environmental performance. The lack of correlation between these evaluations, however, suggests that the students who were most concerned about poor environmental performance were not necessarily the students who were most concerned about other poor lead indicators. We surmise that some third-year students did see environmental performance as an important lead indicator, while others viewed environmental measures as important in their own right. The combination of these two reasons led to the education effect.

Furthermore, the combined effect of the business case (i.e. that environmental performance leads financial performance) and perceived environmental responsibility was greater for third-year students than for experienced controllers. This finding suggests that there is still a gap between the rhetoric of sustainability and its likely implementation in practice. If performance evaluation in organisations ignores poor environmental performance, managers will be receiving mixed signals and positive change is unlikely.

The reasons are not clear for the difference between the weighting placed on environmental performance by third-year students and experienced controllers. The differences between students and controllers may be attributable to factors other than education and experience. For example, on average the students in this study were younger than the controllers. The different emphasis placed on environmental performance may, therefore, be generational. Teasing out these differences would require larger sample sizes. Further research, with more participants, would allow factors such as age and years of experience to be investigated. Alternatively, it could be that, despite their personal views about the importance of environmental performance, experience in organisations led controllers to place less weight on environmental measures. Further research to explore this, perhaps through interviews or other sources of rich data, would address this important question. Furthermore, it would be interesting to compare the organisation's espoused commitment to environmental performance, the accountant's personal attitudes, and their actual decisions.

More encouraging is the finding that education played an important role in providing the understanding necessary to emphasise lead indicators generally, and the strategic importance of environmental performance specifically. Universities have an important role to play in creating a new generation of decision makers who will make a positive difference. As David Orr so aptly stated: 'It is worth noting that [the destruction of the world] is not the work of ignorant people. Rather, it is largely the results of work by people with BAs, BSs, LLBs, MBAs, and PhDs' (Orr, 1994, pp. 7–8). Or, on the positive side: 'the possibilities of changing accounting practices depend just as much on transforming current generations of accounting students' understandings, as on transforming current practitioners, and their understandings' (Day, 1995, p. 104). Similarly, Segovia and Galang (2002, p. 294) argue that 'the university provides an environment that nurtures critical and independent critique of what government or business does'.

An important potential limitation to the generalisability of our results is that our participants were from Australia and Germany. Husted (2005) and Parboteeah, Addae and Cullen (2011) both argue that cultural differences may impact on attitudes toward environmental performance. Although overall social and institutional capacity does not differ significantly between Australia and Germany, specific cultural differences may be important in explaining why environmental performance is, or is not, considered to be strategically important.

According to studies that have used Hofstede's cultural dimensions, Australia is very high on individualism, while Germany is very high on collectivism (Husted, 2005). This has important implications for interpreting the results of this study, since we have assumed an instrumentalist approach in which the importance of environmental performance is based on its anticipated impact on profit. On the other hand, German students and managers may penalise poor environmental performance for reasons other than its impact on profit. For example, Hofstede *et al.* (2002) find that, more than any other country including Australia, MBA students in Germany perceive that responsibilities to employees and society are important goals for successful entrepreneurs. Our study does not allow us to distinguish between these two motives for the weighting placed on environmental performance, which is a limitation of this study and an opportunity for further research.

Regardless of the explanation (profit-linked or societal values), a comparison of evaluations revealed no significant differences between Australian students and German students. Both of these groups of third-year students had received education in which environmental performance was related to economic performance. Note, however, that education for sustainability may be less effective, or require a different approach, in countries that differ significantly from Germany and Australia on important cultural dimensions (Husted, 2005)

What can be seen from this study is that the students were leaving their university with an understanding of the importance of environmental performance. What is not clear, however, is whether experience conflicts with and decreases the concern for environmental performance. Did the controllers in our study enter their careers believing that environmental performance is important but change their view through experience, perhaps because of the values that were implicitly communicated through performance evaluation in their organisations? Will education be able to achieve the desired changes in behaviours when faced with organisational realities? These are important questions for further research, and a longitudinal study is recommended.

References

Adams, C. A., Heijltjes, M. G., Gavin, J., Marjoribanks, T. and Powell, M. (2011) The development of leaders able to respond to climate change and sustainability challenges, *Sustainability Accounting, Management and Policy Journal*, 2, pp. 165–171.

Alewine, H. C. and Stone, D. N. (2009) How does environmental accounting information influence attention and investment? *SSRN eLibrary*. Available at http://dx.doi.org/10.2139/ssrn.1420883

Atwater, J. B. and Pittman, P. H. (2006) Facilitating systematic thinking in business classes, *Decision Sciences Journal of Innovative Education*, 4, pp. 273–292.

Banker, R. D., Chang, H. and Pizzini, M. J. (2004) The balanced scorecard: judgmental effects of performance measures linked to strategy, *The Accounting Review*, 79, pp. 1–23.

Bebbington, J. (1997) Engagement, education and sustainability: a review essay on environmental accounting, *Accounting, Auditing & Accountability*, 10, pp. 365–381.

Bebbington, J., Gray, R., Thomson, I. and Walters, D. (1994) Accountants' attitudes and environmentally-sensitive accounting, *Accounting and Business Research*, 24, pp. 109–120.

Berry, A. and Rondinelli, D. A. (1998) Proactive corporate environment management: a new industrial revolution, *Academy of Management Executive*, 12, pp. 38–50.

Brown, D. L., Dillard, J. F. and Marshall, R. S. (2005) Strategically informed, environmentally conscious information requirements for accounting information systems, *Journal of Information Systems*, 19, pp. 79–103.

Brown, J. and Fraser, M. (2006) Approaches and perspectives in social and environmental accounting: an overview of the conceptual landscape, *Business Strategy and the Environment*, 15, pp. 103–117.

Brunold, A. O. (2006) The United Nations decade of education for sustainable development, its consequences for international political education, and the concept of global learning, *International Education Journal*, 7, pp. 222–234.

Chan, C. C. and Milne, M. J. (1999) Investor reactions to corporate environmental saints and sinners: an experimental analysis, *Accounting and Business Research*, 29, pp. 265–279.

Chen, R. S. (1975) Social and financial stewardship, *The Accounting Review*, 50, pp. 533–543.

Chenhall, R. H. (1997) Reliance on manufacturing performance measures, total quality management and organizational performance, *Management Accounting Research*, 8, pp. 187–206.

Cho, C. H. (2009) Legitimation strategies used in response to environmental disaster: a French case study of Total SA's Erika and AZF incidents, *European Accounting Review*, 18, pp. 33–62.

Cormier, D., Magnan, M. and Van Velthoven, B. (2005) Environmental disclosure quality in large German companies: economic incentives, public pressures or institutional conditions? *European Accounting Review*, 14, pp. 3–39.

Crabtree, A. D. and DeBusk, G. K. (2008) The effects of adopting the balanced scorecard on shareholder returns, *Advances in Accounting*, 24, pp. 8–15.

Csutora, M. (2012) One more awareness gap? The behaviour-impact gap problem, *Journal of Consumer Policy*, 35, pp. 145–163.

Davis, S. and Albright, T. (2004) An investigation of the effect of balanced scorecard implementation on financial performance, *Management Accounting Research*, 15, pp. 135–153.

Day, M. M. (1995) Ethics of teaching critical: feminism on the wings of desire, *Accounting, Auditing & Accountability*, 8, pp. 97–112.

Department of Sustainability, Environment, Water, Population and Communities (1992) *National Strategy for Ecologically Sustainable Development*. Available at http://www.environment.gov.au/about/esd/publications/strategy/index.html

Dilla, W. N. and Steinbart, P. J. (2005) Relative weighting of common and unique balanced scorecard measures by knowledgeable decision makers, *Behavioral Research in Accounting*, 17, pp. 43–53.

Epstein, M. J. and Wisner, P. S. (2001) Using a balanced scorecard to implement sustainability, *Environmental Quality Management*, 11, pp. 1–10.

Figge, F., Hahn, T., Schaltegger, S. and Wagner, M. (2002) The sustainability balanced scorecard – linking sustainability management to business strategy, *Business Strategy and the Environment*, 11, pp. 269–284.

Fisher, J. and Bonn, I. (2011) Business sustainability and undergraduate management education: an Australian study, *Higher Education*, 62, pp. 563–571.

Fleischman, R. K. and Schuele, K. (2006) Green accounting: a primer, *Journal of Accounting Education*, 24, pp. 36–66.

Friedman, M. (1970) The social responsibility of business is to increase its profits, *New York Times Magazine*, September, p. 32.

Gibson, K. (1997) Courses on environmental accounting, *Accounting, Auditing and Accountability Journal*, 10, pp. 584–593.

Global Leaders (2001) *Pilot Environmental Sustainability Index* (Davos: World Economic Forum).

Grablowitz, A., Rudeloff, M. and Voss, G. (2002) A case study on research for sustainable management: the funding priority 'corporate instruments for sustainable management', *International Journal of Sustainability in Higher Education*, 3, pp. 75–82.

Gray, R. (1990) *The Greening of Accountancy: The Profession After Pearce* (London: ACCA).

Hahn, T. and Figge, F. (2011) Beyond the bounded instrumentality in current corporate sustainability research: toward an inclusive notion of profitability, *Journal of Business Ethics*, 104, pp. 325–345.

von der Heidt, T. and Lamberton, G. (2011) Sustainability in the undergraduate and postgraduate business curriculum of a regional university: a critical perspective, *Journal of Management & Organization*, 17, pp. 670–690.

Heskett, J. L., Sasser, W. E. J. and Schlesinger, L. A. (1997) *The Service Profit Chain* (New York: The Free Press).

Hofstede, G., Van Deusen, C. A., Mueller, C. B. and Charles, T. A. (2002) What goals do business leaders pursue? A study of fifteen countries, *International Business Studies*, 33, pp. 785–803.

Hopwood, A. (1972) An empirical study of the role of accounting data in performance evaluation, *Journal of Accounting Research*, 10, pp. 156–182.

Hoque, Z. and James, W. (2000) Linking balanced scorecard measures to size and market factors: impact on organizational performance, *Journal of Management Accounting Research*, 12, pp. 1–17.

Horngren, C. T., Datar, S. M., Foster, G., Rajan, M. V., Ittner, C., Wynder, M., Maguire, W. and Tan, R. (2010) *Cost Accounting: A Managerial Emphasis* (Frenchs Forest, NSW: Pearson).

Husted, B. W. (2005) Culture and ecology: a cross-national study of the determinants of environmental sustainability, *Management International Review*, 45, pp. 349–371.

Ishikawa, K. (1985) *What is Total Quality Control? The Japanese Way* (Englewood Cliffs, NJ: Prentice-Hall).

Ittner, C. D., Larcker, D. F. and Meyer, M. W. (2003) Subjectivity and the weighting of performance measures: evidence from a balanced scorecard, *The Accounting Review*, 78, pp. 725–758.

Jagersma, P. K. (2009) The strategic value of sustainable stakeholder management, *Business Strategy Series*, 10, pp. 339–344.

Johnson, H. T. (1994) Relevance regained: total quality management and the role of management accounting, *Critical Perspectives in Accounting*, 5, pp. 259–267.

Jucker, R. (2002) 'Sustainability? Never heard of it!' Some basics we shouldn't ignore when engaging in education for sustainability, *International Journal of Sustainability in Higher Education*, 3, pp. 8–18.

Kaplan, R. and Norton, D. (1993) Putting the balanced scorecard to work, *Harvard Business Review*, 71, pp. 134–142.

Kaplan, R. and Norton, D. (1996) *The Balanced Scorecard* (Boston, MA: Harvard Business School Press).

Kaplan, R. and Norton, D. (2000) *The Strategy-focused Organisation* (Boston: Harvard Business School Press).

Kaplan, S. E. and Wisner, P. S. (2009) The judgmental effects of management communications and a fifth balanced scorecard category on performance evaluation, *Behavioral Research in Accounting*, 21, pp. 37–56.

Kelly, M. and Alam, M. (2009) Educating accounting students in an age of sustainability, *The Australasian Accounting Business and Finance Journal*, 3, pp. 30–44.

Kollmuss, A. and Agyemann, J. (2002) Mind the gap: why do people act environmentally and what are the barriers to pro-environmental behavior? *Environmental Education Research*, 8, pp. 239–260.

Langfield-Smith, K., Thorne, H. and Hilton, R. W. (2012) *Mangement Accounting: Information for Creating and Managing Value* (Sydney: McGraw-Hill Australia).

Lee, D., Faff, R. and Langfield-Smith, K. (2009) Revisiting the vexing question: does superior corporate social performance lead to improved financial performance? *Australian Journal of Management*, 34, pp. 21–49.

Lei, D., Slocum, J. W. and Pitts, R. A. (1999) Designing organizations for competitive advantage: the power of unlearning and learning, *Organizational Dynamics*, 27, pp. 24–38.

Libby, T., Salterio, S. E. and Webb, A. (2004) The balanced scorecard: the effects of assurance and process accountability on managerial judgement, *The Accounting Review*, 79, pp. 1075–1094.

Liedtka, S. L., Church, B. K. and Ray, M. R. (2008) Performance variability, ambiguity intolerance, and balanced scorecard-based performance assessments, *Behavioral Research in Accounting*, 20, pp. 73–88.

Lipe, M. G. and Salterio, S. E. (2000) The balanced scorecard: judgmental effects of common and unique performance measures, *The Accounting Review*, 75, pp. 283–298.

Lipe, M. G. and Salterio, S. E. (2002) A note on the judgmental effects of the balanced scorecard's information organization, *Accounting, Organizations and Society*, 27, pp. 531–540.

Luther, D. B. (1992) Advanced TQM: measurements, missteps, and progress through key result indicators at Corning, *National Productivity Review*, 12, pp. 23.

MacVaugh, J. and Norton, M. (2012) Introducing sustainability into business education contexts using active learning, *International Journal of Sustainability in Higher Education*, 13, pp. 72–87.

Maunders, K. T. and Burritt, R. L. (1991) Accounting and ecological crisis, *Accounting, Auditing and Accountability Journal*, 4, pp. 9–26.

McWilliams, A. and Siegel, D. (2000) Corporate social responsibility and financial performance: correlation or misspecification? *Strategic Management Journal*, 21, pp. 603–609.

Molina-Azorín, J. F., Claver-Cortés, E., López-Gamero, M. D. and Tarí, J. J. (2009) Green management and financial performance: a literature review, *Management Decision*, 47, pp. 1080–1100.

Moller, A. and Schaltegger, S. (2005) The sustainability balanced scorecard as a framework for eco-efficiency analysis, *Journal of Industrial Ecology*, 9, pp. 73–83.

Naeem, M. and Neal, M. (2011) Sustainability in business education in the Asia Pacific region: a snapshot of the situation, *International Journal of Sustainability in Higher Education*, 13, pp. 60–71.

Orr, D. W. (1994) *Earth in Mind: On Education, Environment, and the Human Prospect* (Washington, DC: Island Press).

Parboteeah, K. P., Addae, H. M. and Cullen, J. B. (2011) Propensity to support sustainability initiatives: a cross-national model, *Journal of Business Ethics*, 105, pp. 401–413.

Peloza, J. (2009) The challenge of measuring financial impacts from investments in corporate social performance, *Journal of Management Accounting Research*, 35, pp. 1518–1541.

Rennie, M. and Gibbins, M. (1993) Expert beyond experience, *CA Magazine*, 126, pp. 40–46.

Rikhardsson, P. and Holm, C. (2008) The effect of environmental information on investment allocation decisions – an experimental study, *Business Strategy and the Environment*, 17, pp. 382–397.

Samson, D. and Terziovski, M. (1999) The relationship between total quality management practices and operational performance, *Journal of Operations Management*, 17, pp. 393–409.

Schreck, P. (2011) Reviewing the business case for corporate social responsibility: new evidence and analysis, *Journal of Business Ethics*, 103, pp. 167–188.

Segovia, V. M. and Galang, A. P. (2002) Sustainable development in higher education in the Philippines – the case of Miriam College, *International Journal of Sustainability in Higher Education*, 3, pp. 288–296.

Shank, J. K. and Govindarajan, V. (1994) Measuring 'Cost of Quality': a strategic cost management perspective, *Journal of Cost Management*, Summer, pp. 5–17.

Speckbacher, G., Bischof, J. and Pfeiffer, T. (2003) A descriptive analysis of the implementation of balanced scorecards in German-speaking countries, *Management Accounting Research*, 14, pp. 361–388.

Thomas, I. (2004) Sustainability in tertiary curricula: what is stopping it happening? *International Journal of Sustainability in Higher Education*, 5, pp. 33–47.

Touche Ross Management Consultants (1990) *Heads in the Clouds or Heads in the Sand? UK Manager Attitudes to Environmental Issues* (London: Touche Ross).

UNESCO (2005) *United Nations Decade of Education for Sustainable Development 2005-2014* (Paris: UNESCO).

Wheeler, D. and Elkington, J. (2001) The end of the corporate environmental report? Or the advent of cybernetic sustainability reporting and communication, *Business Strategy and the Environment*, 10, pp. 1–14.

Wong-On-Wing, B., Guo, L., Li, W. and Yang, D. (2007) Reducing conflict in balanced scorecard evaluations, *Accounting, Organizations and Society*, 32, pp. 363–377.

Wynder, M. B. (2011) Chemico: evaluating performance based on the balanced scorecard, *Journal of Accounting Education*, 28, pp. 221–236.

Zsóka, Á. (2005) *Consistency and Awareness Gaps in Pro-Environmental Organisational Behaviour* (Budapest: Corvinus University of Budapest).

who were asked to assess the performance of three managers. Wynder, Wellner and Reinhard (2013) found in the experiment that education positively influences a longer-term perspective and the consideration of environmental indicators. However, they also found that professional experience does not make any difference in terms of the adoption of a longer-term perspective and, more revealing, goes against the consideration of environmental performance in manager evaluation. In the remainder of this Commentary I will concentrate on environmental performance, which is the focus of the paper.

Wynder, Wellner and Reinhard (2013) take for granted the existence of a business case for investing in social and environmental performance and take the view that education provides a better understanding of such a business case than does experience. But assuming that there exists a business case, one question that the study raises is why it is the case that education reveals the business case more effectively than does practice; because it seems very unlikely that experienced controllers can be systematically wrong. Can we realistically assume that controllers 'do not understand or believe that environmental performance is strategically important' (p. 377)? A different (less tortuous) interpretation of the findings could be that we think that a business case is desirable and educate students accordingly, but in most cases a business case for environmental protection does not emerge in practice. This rationale is consistent with the first view of the interplay between sustainability and business decision-making mentioned earlier. Whereas 'the notion that business will do things because they make business sense is itself hardly surprising' (Spence, 2007, p. 874), Gray (2006) contends that the existence of a business case can only be sustained if we choose to ignore the social and environmental state of the planet and how notions of economic success are intertwined with higher levels of waste and consumption. Following this rationale, it could be argued that the results of this experiment are consistent with the notion that the education of students in the business case for environmental protection is effective *and* with the *absence* of such a business case in *practice*.

The existence of a business case for environmental protection is a desire, a normative proposition that has some merit because it is effective in the education process, but which is probably ineffective by itself in changing business practice. In this regard, although the influence of education revealed in the study is encouraging, the crux of the matter is why and how education is not being effective in the transformation of praxis. Is there any lag effect of present education on future praxis? Wynder, Wellner and Reinhard (2013) seem to be pointing to this argument when they signal that students are, on average, younger than controllers. This would be an optimistic prognosis. Is there a divorce between individuals' reactions in an education/normative setting and their reactions in a business/practice setting? Wynder, Wellner and Reinhard (2013) conjecture that, despite their personal views (education?), controllers' experiences in organizations might lead them to play down environmental indicators. Explaining this situation and exploring new avenues for change are urgent areas of research. The results reported in this paper invite us to further reflect on the role of education in a change for sustainability.

One of the areas that requires further reflection is the education process itself. Thomson and Bebbington (2004) provide some insight in to this with their discussion about the relative importance of education *content* and education *methods*. They argue that simply depositing new issues (e.g. the business case for sustainability) in passive students who have incentives to replicate this material in assessment to obtain grades (i.e. a traditional 'banking' education system) will be ineffective in the transformation of praxis. Following this rationale, I would argue that passive students, who succeed to obtain grades showing competence in the replication of rules that are prevailing in education (e.g. business case), will do in practice what makes business sense, according to the set of rules that are prevailing in actual performance measurement, which, according to Gray (2006), unfortunately is not likely to take into consideration its social and environmental consequences.

In conclusion, the study reported in Wynder, Wellner and Reinhard (2013) provides very interesting insight, allowing a diversity of interpretations from the more managerial, based on the business case, to the more critical, the focus of which is on the explanation of inertia and change. Moreover, these results invite further reflection on how to educate business managers to deal ethically with sustainability issues. This will probably require opening the education black box and questioning not only its content but also its methods along the lines suggested, for example, by Thomson and Bebbington (2004).

References

Adams, C. A. (2002) Internal organisational factors influencing corporate social and ethical reporting: beyond current theorising, *Accounting, Auditing & Accountability Journal*, 15(2), pp. 223–250.

Bebbington, J., Brown, J. *et al.* (2007) Theorizing engagement: the potential of a critical dialogic approach, *Accounting, Auditing & Accountability Journal*, 20(3), pp. 356–381.

Gray, R. (2006) Social, environmental and sustainability reporting and organisational value creation? Whose value? Whose creation? *Accounting, Auditing & Accountability Journal*, 19(6), pp. 793–819.

Husillos, J. and Álvarez, M. J. (2008) A stakeholder-theory approach to environmental disclosures by small and medium enterprises, *Spanish Accounting Review*, 11(1), pp. 125–156.

Owen, D. (2008) Chronicles of wasted time? A personal reflection on the current state of, and future prospects for, social and environmental accounting research, *Accounting, Auditing & Accountability Journal*, 21(2), pp. 240–267.

Spence, C. (2007) Social and environmental reporting and hegemonic discourse, *Accounting, Auditing and Accountability Journal*, 20(6), pp. 855–882.

Thomson, I. and Bebbington, J. (2004) It doesn't matter what you teach?, *Critical Perspectives on Accounting*, 15(4–5), pp. 609–628.

Wynder, M., Wellner, K.-U. and Reinhard, K. (2013) Rhetoric or reality? Do accounting education and experience increase weighting on environmental performance in a balanced scorecard?, *Accounting Education: An International Journal*, 22(4), pp. 366–381.

crowd out educational effects. Such an interpretation would require a research design that distinguishes different kinds of education, experience and business settings, and ideally be longitudinal.

No doubt, the use of experiments as a research method has delivered good results in various areas and is a recommendable path for future empirical research on the effects and effectiveness of sustainability accounting approaches and education. However, to receive robust results the research design is crucial and further differentiated studies are needed. This includes additional independent variables such as the *kind of education*, the *kind of accounting tool with which environmental preference is expressed*, and the *setting in which practical experiences are gained*. The question whether, to what extent, and in which direction education and experience can change attitudes and behaviour may be influenced by what is taught and the business setting of experience.

Accounting, environmental and sustainability education may differ in rhetoric and thematic emphasis, which can be expected to substantially influence the outcome of an experiment. According to the *critical school, the role of business and accounting education is to critique the capitalist paradigm* (e.g. Bebbington *et al.*, 1997). Such an education either suggests not entering corporate practice at all to evade mind-corrupting structures, or otherwise, when choosing a business career, to believe that destroying the environment is an inevitable fate connected with making money and thus it is not possible to give environmental performance significant weight in corporate practice. If *students are taught* that it is impossible for managers to consider environmental goals in practice because of structural obstacles, it would not be logical to expect managers to change their behaviour to increase environmental performance and at the same time the financial performance of the company. Similarly, abstract sustainability courses dealing with broad macro-level issues may leave students with the feeling of inability over how to create change. Practical experience based on such an educational background can be expected to lead to low weighting of environmental performance indicators and measures as part of a *self-fulfilling prophecy*.

As a difference, business and accounting education can also be *designed to support 'change agents for sustainability' in exploring possible solutions* to environmental and social problems and in overcoming obstacles of structural rigidity. This kind of education sees managers as being competent key agents of change for sustainable development and emphazises the design and application of sustainability management methods, approaches to overcome concrete organizational barriers, and case studies on how to succeed in implementing more sustainable business practices (e.g. Schaltegger and Burritt, 2010). As a consequence, the expectation can be formulated that sustainability management and accounting courses teaching how to organize change processes that are informed by *examples of entrepreneurs who have succeeded with more sustainable businesses* would change attitudes and behaviour towards weighing environmental performance higher.

In summary, if students are effectively educated to believe that pursuing social and environmental goals is always at the cost of economic performance and vice versa, then third-year students are likely to weigh environmental performance highly, but when becoming a practitioner, to underscore environmental goals as this would contradict their decision to work for business. In contrast, third-year students and practitioners effectively educated in pragmatic sustainability accounting and processes of solution creation to realize business cases for sustainability are more likely to weigh environmental performance highly at the end of their studies and in business context experiences while at the same time securing economic performance.

This leads to the question: 'What students with which *background* and what *teaching materials* are part of the study?' Sustainability is increasingly considered in conventional management accounting books (e.g. Horngren *et al.*, 2010), but sustainability accounting is also dealt with in sustainability management textbooks and in specific environmental accounting books (e.g. Schaltegger and Burritt, 2000; Schaltegger, Burritt and Petersen, 2003). Depending on whether accounting, management or environmental science students are taught in sustainability accounting with what kind of textbook materials, different learning outcomes may result. Students with different graduation degrees may also enter different kinds of jobs in different departments of companies (e.g. the accounting or sustainability department) and other organizations (e.g. consulting, NGO or industry) or work on different management levels (top or middle management), thus facing different experience settings. Most crucial may be whether the interviewed practitioners are exposed to substantial sustainability pressures, working in innovative sustainability business fields (e.g. in the renewable energy sector, which profits economically from an environmental focus), or whether they work in companies known as sustainability laggards (e.g. a coal-based energy utility which faces costs of end-of-pipe technologies).

A crucial question for further research is thus what kind of accounting and sustainability education the students receive and what kind of experiences former students make in which business contexts when becoming practitioners.

References

Bebbington, J. (1997) Engagement, education and sustainability. A review essay on environmental accounting, *Accounting, Auditing and Accountability Journal*, 10(3), pp. 365–381.

Bebbington, J., Gray, R., Thomson, I. and Walters, D. (1994) Accountants' attitudes and environmentally-sensitive accounting, *Accounting and Business Research*, 24, pp. 109–120.

Burritt, R. and Schaltegger, S. (2010) Sustainability accounting and reporting: fad or trend? *Accounting, Auditing and Accountability Journal*, 23(7), pp. 829–846.

Gray, R. (1990) *The Greening of Accountancy: The Profession After Pearce* (London: ACCA).

Hopwood, A., Unermann, J. and Fries, J. (2012) *Accounting for Sustainability. Practical Insights* (London: Earthscan).

Horngren, C. T., Datar, S. M., Foster, G., Rajan, M. V., Ittner, C., Wynder, M., Maguire, W. and Tan, R. (2010) *Cost Accounting: A Managerial Emphasis* (Frenchs Forest, NSW: Pearson).

Schaltegger, S. and Burritt, R. (2000) *Contemporary Environmental Accounting* (Sheffield: Greenleaf).

Schaltegger, S. and Burritt, R. (2010) Sustainability for companies. Catchphrase or decision support for business leaders? *Journal of World Business*, 45(4), pp. 375–384.

Schaltegger, S., Burritt, R. and Petersen, H. (2003) *An Introduction to Corporate Environmental Management: Striving for Sustainability* (Sheffield: Greenleaf).

Wynder, M., Wellner, K.-U. and Reinhard, K. (2013) Rhetoric or reality? Do accounting education and experience increase weighting on environmental performance in a balanced scorecard?, *Accounting Education: An International Journal*, 22(4), pp. 366–381.

Premise 2: Social and environmental performance often impacts on economic performance, but in ways that may be difficult to understand and predict.

Premise 3: Understanding the why *and the how* are both necessary to translate vague commitments toward social and environmental responsibility into effective action.

Conclusion 1: Accounting education has an important role to play in changing attitudes and driving behaviour by providing philosophical and economic rationales.

Conclusion 2. For attitudes to lead to effective action, graduates must have the analytic and calculative tools to manage social and environmental performance.

These premises and conclusions are certainly not without challenge. For example, our findings suggest that experienced controllers do not view environmental performance as being the responsibility of, or economically important to, profit-seeking organisations. This might cause some to argue against incorporating sustainability into the accounting curriculum. This begs the question, however, whether education should mirror practice, or seek to influence it. We view the gap between education and praxis as a call for further research.

Ibrahim, Angelidis and Howard (2006) find that practising accountants are less responsive to corporate social responsibility than are accounting students. They attribute their finding to an increased emphasis on economic performance, arguing that 'the maturity and experience of practicing accountants provide a greater appreciation of the business world's economic "realities"' (p. 162). An alternative view is that there is a reality that is obscured by existing accounting practice. As noted by Raiborn, Butler and Massoud (2011, p. 429): 'It can, therefore, be inferred that some portion of business' lack of emphasis on environmental responsibility is, in part, an inevitable result of the way accountants account for organizational activities'. Furthermore, they argue that material long-term risks and benefits are ignored when environmental considerations are not incorporated into the formal reporting structures.

Understanding *why* practitioners in our study did not weight environmental performance in their evaluations is important in bringing about the change that we advocate. We conjecture that it can be attributed to both attitude and understanding. Changing attitudes is insufficient if individuals do not have the understanding necessary to justify and achieve social and environmental objectives. Distinguishing between these two potential causes of inaction offers a fruitful avenue for further research because changing attitudes and increasing understanding may be achieved in different ways.

If change in practice is to occur, it will begin with education. Therefore, integrating social and environmental performance objectives throughout the accounting curriculum is critical. Many accounting theory texts (e.g. Gaffikin, 2008) discuss the role of corporate social responsibility within the broader framework of the nature and role of the modern organisation. Providing a philosophical argument for social and environmental objectives is important, but insufficient. Providing a causal model, in the form of a strategy map, seems to be effective in increasing managers' understanding of the strategic drivers of performance (Cheng and Humphreys, 2012). Similarly, students are more likely to understand the strategic importance of social and environmental performance when it is incorporated into causal models, such as the balanced scorecard, and illustrated in the form of a strategy map (e.g. Wynder, 2011). Such mental models may also be important in creating a persistent impact by providing a framework through which graduates can interpret the results that they observe in practice.

It is also important that educators provide graduates with the skills and tools necessary to manage social and environmental performance. Management accounting texts (e.g. Langfield-Smith, Thorne and Hilton, 2009; Horngren *et al.*, 2011) demonstrate how traditional tools, such as activity-based management and capital budgeting, can be used to support social and environmental objectives.

In summary, the position advanced in this Rejoinder is that philosophical arguments for social and environmental performance are important and should be incorporated in accounting education. Economic rationales are also useful and important, however, for at least two reasons. Economic justification is an important part of satisfying an organisation's fiduciary duty to shareholders, which is critical to obtaining the economic resources necessary for sustainable operations. Understanding *how* social and environmental objectives are achieved is also necessary. Traditional management accounting techniques provide tools that can be used to simultaneously, or separately, support the achievement of social, environmental and economic objectives. In other words, understanding drivers, and managing limited resources, is necessary for organisations to get the most social and environmental bang for their buck.

Note

[1] Although our research focused on environmental performance, the broad issues discussed in this Rejoinder apply equally to social objectives.

References

Cheng, M. M. and Humphreys, K. A. (2012) The differential improvement effects of the Strategy Map and scorecard perspectives on managers' strategic judgments, *The Accounting Review*, 87(3), pp. 899–924.

Gaffikin, M. (2008) *Accounting Theory: Research, Regulation and Accounting Practice* (Frenchs Forest: Pearson Education Australia).

Gibson, K. (2012) Stakeholder and sustainability: an evolving theory, *Journal of Business Ethics*, 109, pp. 15–25.

Horngren, C. T., Datar, S. M., Foster, G., Rajan, M. V., Ittner, C., Wynder, M., Maguire, W. and Tan, R. (2010) *Cost Accounting: A Managerial Emphasis* (Frenchs Forest, NSW, Pearson).

Ibrahim, N. A., Angelidis, J. P. and Howard, D. P. (2006) Corporate social responsibility: a comparative analysis of perceptions of practicing accountants and accounting students, *Journal of Business Ethics*, 66(2/3), pp. 157–167.

Langfield-Smith, K., Thorne, H. and Hilton, R. (2009) *Management Accounting: Information for Creating and Managing Value* (Sydney: McGraw-Hill).

Larrinaga, C. (2013) A commentary on 'Rhetoric or reality? Do accounting education and experience increase weighting on environmental performance in a balanced scorecard?', *Accounting Education: An International Journal*, 22(4), pp. 382–384.

Raiborn, C. A., Butler, J. B. and Massoud, M. F. (2011) Environmental reporting: toward enhanced information quality, *Business Horizons*, 54, pp. 425–433.

Schaltegger, S. (2013) Sustainability education and accounting experience. What motivates higher valuation of environmental performance? *Accounting Education: An International Journal*, 22(4), pp. 385–387.

Wynder, M. B. (2011) Chemico: evaluating performance based on the balanced scorecard, *Journal of Accounting Education*, 28, pp. 221–236.

Wynder, M., Wellner, K.-U. and Reinhard, K. (2013) Rhetoric or reality? Do accounting education and experience increase weighting on environmental performance in a balanced scorecard? *Accounting Education: An International Journal*, 22(4), pp. 366–381.

every organ of society, keeping this Declaration constantly in mind, *shall strive by teaching and education to promote respect for these rights* and freedoms and by progressive measures, national and international, to secure their universal and effective recognition and observance, both among the peoples of Member States themselves and among the peoples of territories under their jurisdiction. (Preamble of the Universal Declaration on Human Rights; United Nations, 1948, emphasis added)

1. Introduction

The human rights discourse has become *the* generally accepted global normative standard for the way human beings should be treated (Howen, 2005) by all organs of society, including businesses. A report by the Business Leaders Initiative on Human Rights (2004) commented that:

> increased numbers of businesses [are] willing to talk seriously about their human rights responsibilities, perhaps recognizing that human rights is the most legitimate and universal framework for determining the social dimensions of business responsibility and issues of corporate governance. (BLIHR, 2004, p. 11)

In the past decade the normative standards of human rights have increasingly been applied to the activities of multinational corporations (MNCs) rather than nation states. MNCs are now perceived to be able to positively and negatively impact on the recognition and observance of human rights across the globe. There are a number of reasons for this. These include the growing economic significance of corporations (Korten, 2001; Rugman, 2005); evidence of corporate involvement in human rights violation; and changes in the dynamic between the state and business, with many public services (such as health care, education, and security) now delivered by private corporations. The rise of the MNC has been accompanied with a diminution of the power of the nation state, which traditionally was the organ of society with the duty and responsibility to prevent human rights abuse. The growing economic power of MNCs has not always been accompanied with a growth in their concern with human rights. The United Nations named 85 companies (18 based in the UK) that helped perpetuate human rights abuses in the Democratic Republic of Congo (Christian Aid, 2005).[1] Ratner (2001, p. 446) concludes that:

> The last decade has witnessed a striking new phenomenon in strategies to protect human rights: a shift by global actors concerned about human rights from nearly exclusive attention on the abuses committed by governments to close scrutiny of the activities of business enterprises, in particular multinational corporations.

These problematic developments, combined with the *Universal Declaration on Human Rights'* call to every organ of society to educate for the promotion of human rights, would appear to create a compelling case to critically explore whether and how corporate responsibilities for human rights should be incorporated into accounting and business education.

The majority of research and education on the human rights responsibilities of corporations has been undertaken within law schools rather than business schools. This increased concern with the relationship between corporations and human rights has been almost completely overlooked within the accounting research literature,[2,3] although there is a growing body of work in the business ethics field (Nolan, 2009; Seppala, 2009; Whelan, Moon and Orlitzky, 2009; Wettstein, 2010; Macdonald, 2011). This absence seems surprising given the renewed focus on ethics within the accounting profession, including the International Federation of Accountants' (IFAC) attempt to develop a universal code of ethics for all professional accountants (Farrell and Cobbin, 2000; Clements, Neill and Stovall, 2009). It would appear that the universal language of professional integrity remains largely disconnected from the possibility of accounting's complicity in human rights abuses.

This paper contends that the emergence of the language of human rights into the global discourse on corporate accountability represents a significant development in the practice and discourse of corporate governance, which requires a substantive response from accounting and business educators.

The paper takes its orientation from the critical accounting literature (for example, Entwistle, 1979; Giroux, 1983; Aronowitz and Giroux, 1991; Dillard 1991; Lewis, Humphrey and Owen, 1992; Gray, Bebbington and McPhail, 1994; Gallhofer and Haslam, 1996; McPhail, 2001a; Poullaos, 2004) and draws attention to the need for a critical discussion of how the ideal of human rights and regulatory assumptions of corporations' roles in promoting human rights (Douzinas, 2000, 2007) can be incorporated into business and professional accounting curricula. Rather than advocating unquestioning support for corporate responsibilities for human rights, or the ideological underpinnings of universal human rights, this paper calls for a critical reflection on whether and how the human rights discourse could contribute towards more just and equitable forms of accounting practice. The paper argues that students should be encouraged to critically engage with the ideological proposition that corporations and accounting can support the realization of the *Universal Declaration on Human Rights* (United Nations, 1948), but this paper does not seek to prescribe or pre-empt the outcome of this critical engagement.

The paper argues that a critical consideration of human rights should be incorporated into accounting and sustainability educational discourses and practices (Gray, Bebbington and McPhail, 1994). It was recognized at the 1972 United Nations (UN) conference on the Human Environment in Stockholm that the state of the environment and the realization of human rights are interconnected. This conference acknowledged that the environment is essential to human 'wellbeing and to the enjoyment of basic human rights even the right to life itself' (NGLS, 2002, p. 2). Since then the alignment of the environmental and human rights discourse has been problematic, with a number of areas of conflict. The discourse on rights has brought the rights of the corporation, for example, in relation to foreign direct investment, into conflict with environmental legislation (Sikka, 2011), while others question whether the realization of basic human rights is environmentally sustainable (Vischer, 2005).

The concerns of this paper are as follows. Firstly, that accounting and business curricula have yet to critically engage with the emerging discourse on business and human rights and their disparate ideological underpinnings.[4] Secondly, that social and environmental accounting education has thus far overlooked the notion of human rights. There appears to be a need for accounting and business education to critically engage with the relationships amongst human rights, sustainability, corporate governance and corporate accountability. While the emerging discourse on business and human rights has clear implications for internal accounting systems and external disclosure requirements, it also raises questions about the broader frameworks of accountability on which much accounting education is predicated and how corporations could be reflexively re-constituted in the act of rendering accounts for human rights (Arrington and Francis, 1993; Schweiker, 1993; Shearer, 2002).

The remainder of the paper is structured as follows. Section 2 explores the current lack of attention to human rights within accounting, business and professional education, and considers what an appropriate business education program for human rights might involve.

Section 3 briefly introduces the emerging discourse on business and human rights. Section 4 considers how this discourse is being translated into business practice. Sections 3 and 4 are not intended to provide normative support for these developments, rather they highlight the extent to which human rights is emerging as the predominant social norm against which business practice is to be held accountable. These sections identify how this norm is emerging in institutional reforms and changes in business and accounting practices, thus highlighting areas for critical reflection. Section 5 explores the relationship between sustainability and human rights. Concluding remarks are provided in Section 6.

2. Accounting Education and Human Rights.

There is a growing awareness of the increasing size and power of MNCs and the inability of nation states to discipline companies for breaches of human rights that fall outside their jurisdiction. The geo-political shift in the global economy now means that MNCs work across national boundaries and may not be subject to the laws of the countries in which they operate. MNCs are able to benefit from complicity in human rights abuses but also have the power to influence countries to improve their poor human rights records. Unfortunately there is very little evidence of MNCs acting in a positive fashion and a growing number of cases in which MNCs have been complicit in human rights violations. The increased visibility of the relationship between MNCs and human rights, accompanied with an increasing role for corporations in the provision of state services, has resulted in a raft of international initiatives, standards and protocols that seek to change the problematic relationship between corporations and human rights. As a result the human rights discourse is slowly entering the narrative of corporate social responsibility, corporate governance and corporate accountability. Despite these changes there seems to be little discussion about business, human rights and sustainability in relation to the processes and practices of business and accounting education. Anecdotal evidence suggests that there are very low levels of human rights and sustainability content in the curricula of business schools, accounting departments, or professional accounting programs. It would be interesting to know how many university signatories to UN Global Compact initiatives have human rights courses as compulsory elements of their business and accounting curricula. It would appear that human rights *will not* be incorporated into the mindset of future accountants or business leaders without significant changes in business school educational programs or the aculturalization processes of the accounting professions.

However, building a case for incorporating human rights into accounting and business education is not difficult. There are two main dimensions to this case: the moral argument and the pragmatic argument. The moral argument builds from the notion that if human rights represent a way of protecting the most vulnerable from abuse and exploitation, then we should be concerned with all 'organs in society' that can affect the promotion and violation of human rights. Given the contemporary power of corporations to both positively and negatively impact on human rights, morally human rights should form part of all aspects of education associated with corporate governance and practices.

There is also the pragmatic argument. If business schools want to prepare students adequately for the kinds of issues that will populate their professional life world, then they should be critically aware of human rights. As Ratner (2001) commented, the recognition by corporations of their human rights responsibilities undercuts any ideological or doctrinal bar to human right education. The observable fact that the human rights discourse is a significant and growing part of corporations' policy, practice and reporting would appear to negate any objections from business schools that human rights fall beyond the scope of business and accounting education. These objections can also be challenged by the observation that contemporary business and accounting education is already rights based, but only concerned with the human rights of a particular group, namely shareholders' property rights (Chang, 2002).

This paper is premised on the assumption that the purpose of university business schools is to provide the space and the capacity for critical reflection on key social issues, not just to develop students' technical understanding of corporate social responsibility (CSR) or to inculcate an unquestioning respect for official statements of human rights in future business leaders. It would seem that we are entering a critically important period in the ideological construction of rights as they apply to states, corporations and individuals. If the human rights discourse is to play an important role in ensuring human dignity is not sacrificed in the pursuit of economic development, then it is crucial that human rights receive considerably more critical analysis and coverage in accounting and business curricula. When attempting to incorporate any kind of rights into business and accounting educational programs it should be from the basic understanding that all rights are political and ideological concepts.

An even stronger case can be made for incorporating critical awareness of human rights in professional accounting curricula. One would imagine that ensuring human rights are respected, protected and promoted would be central to any claim by the accountancy profession to act in the public interest. One would expect that the renaissance in professional ethics, both within the accounting profession and other professions, would incorporate a critical reflection on the emerging human rights discourse. Unfortunately the accountancy profession has, in the past, responded to periods of public scrutiny in ways that serve its own rather than the public interest (Sikka, Willmott and Lowe, 1989; Walker 1988, 1991). A critical awareness of human rights could be used to reflect on what the profession's claim to the (global) public interest might mean, particularly as financial reporting standards become internationally accepted and accounting's centrality to global financial systems increases. This critical examination could compare the underlying neo-liberal framework and the rights currently served by standards of the International Accounting Standards Board (IASB) with the contemporary human rights discourse. The IASB has been involved in a number of debates concerning conflicts between commercial rights and human rights. One example was the failed attempts by the Tax Justice Network and Christian Aid to get a tax reporting requirement incorporated into the IASB's segmental reporting standard.[5]

If it is accepted that human rights should be incorporated into accounting education programs, then we need to explore what a human rights-informed accounting curriculum would look like and how it would be taught. As mentioned previously, the objective of this paper is not to prescribe a definitive human rights accounting curriculum, but rather to set out the case for the inclusion of human rights within business and accounting curricula; to link human rights with sustainability; to use human rights to frame our analysis of professional accounting bodies and global bodies like IFAC; and to raise issues for further reflection. There is a burgeoning literature on the content and delivery styles of effective business and accounting learning, which lies beyond the scope of this paper.

The development of curricula for business, accounting and human rights should not be undertaken just by accountants or accounting academics. If these curricula are to have any external legitimacy these should be developed in conjunction with organizations such as the International Labor Organization (ILO), Christian Aid, Amnesty International and Human Rights Watch, and representatives from the UN Working Group on Business and Human Rights. The process of developing human rights curricula for business and accounting is critical to its pedagogic effectiveness, whether for global professional bodies such as IFAC, national accountancy institutes, or business schools.

Whatever the content of a business, accounting and human rights curriculum, it is important that students are given a sense of how current business practice is already about rights, primarily shareholders' property rights and corporations' intellectual and property rights, and how these rights are supported in law due to the structural power of corporations and capital owners. Students also need to be given a sense of how businesses and broader economic systems are connected to human rights issues and how corporations can adversely (and positively) impact on the realization of human rights and the pursuit of environmental sustainability.

These learning objectives go some way towards dispelling two firmly entrenched myths about accounting and business practice. Firstly, they would challenge the myth that accounting and business practice is amoral. Secondly, the human rights discourse challenges the outmoded doctrine, taught in many business schools, that the sole function of business is to maximize shareholder wealth. It is crucially important that the issue of human rights is not cast as just another risk that needs to be managed, as to do so would miss the structural tensions that represent the core challenges of bringing the discourse of human rights to bear on the practice of business. Venkateswarlu (2007, p. 9), for example, commented that:

> The wage rates for children are far lower than adult wages. We can reduce our labour costs considerably if we hire girl children. If we want to hire adult labour we have to pay higher wages. With the current procurement price we get from the seed companies we cannot afford to pay higher wages to the labourers. The exploitation of child labour on cottonseed farms is linked to larger market forces. Several large-scale national and multinational seed companies, which produce and market the seeds, are involved in perpetuating the problem of child labour. The economic relationship behind this abuse is multi-tiered and complex and masks legal and social responsibility.

A business and human rights curriculum would need to address the extent to which corporate complicity in human rights violations is related to the structural conditions of the global economic system and the subsequent tensions that may arise between development rights and environmental rights. In relation to the United Nations Education, Scientific and Cultural Organisation (UNESCO) Tbilisi conference, Wright (2002) commented:

> The participants at this conference felt that radical social change must occur before environmental change can transpire. The declaration also recognized that sustainability initiatives must take place at all levels of society and must be interdisciplinary in nature. The declaration argued that the concept of environmental sustainability must be clearly linked with poverty, population, food security, democracy, human rights, peace and health and a respect for traditional cultural and ecological knowledge.

Tilbury et al. (2002, p. 21) similarly commented on how 'education about bio-diversity (and other nature-based themes) now needs to be immersed in concepts of human rights, equity and democracy, which are the core issues of sustainability (Fien, 1993)'.

It is argued that, while a response to these challenges may lie to some extent in the moral integrity of individuals (and if enough individuals responded in a moral way, then substantive change might occur), there is also a pressing requirement for greater engagement with the systemic nature of business complicity in human rights abuses in order to construct innovative, systemic and regulatory solutions. In order to build future capacity to enable these innovative solutions to emerge, business and accounting students need to participate in the human rights discourse and engage in developing solutions as part of their educational experience.

A review of the emerging business and human rights discourse suggests that a critical accounting and human rights curriculum might include:

- the nature of human rights, human rights law, and how the business and human rights discourse impacts on our notions of corporate accountability;
- the ways corporations impact on human rights and whether or not accounting systems make it easier for human rights to be violated;
- the relationship between sustainability and human rights;
- the extent to which business responsibility for human rights is underpinned by a neo-liberal ideology; and
- the extent to which the global economic system creates tensions amongst the competing rights of property owners, laborers and others.

It is important for the human rights content in business and accounting education programs to contain a critique of the socially constructed nature of human rights discourses. Douzinas (2007) casts the human rights discourse as a form of neo-imperialism that serves the cultural and economic interests of the West. A point underlined by the decision of the Organisation of the Islamic Conference (OIC) to adopt their own Declaration on Human Rights in Islam (OIC, 1990) as a response to the perceived Western bias in the Universal Declaration of Human Rights.

Introducing human rights into accounting and business curricula requires decisions to be made about what to jettison from already overcrowded educational programs. These decisions might involve critical reflections on the relevance of the knowledge currently taught or content that could be more effectively delivered via different learning mechanisms. Perhaps the greater challenge is not how to fit human rights into existing curricula, but rather how to ensure it will have some substantive impact on students' perceptions of business and the potential of accounting to contribute towards a just economic and social order (McPhail, 2001b).

The following two sections outline the evolution of the connection between business and human rights, from their conceptual underpinnings to how these ideas are beginning to impinge upon everyday business practice. This discussion provides the basis for a more explicit engagement with the complex inter-relationship between human rights and sustainability.

3.   The Emerging Discourse on Business and Human Rights

This section briefly reviews the evolving business and human rights policy agenda, building from the 1948 *Universal Declaration on Human Rights* and traditional human rights responsibilities of nation states to discuss the contemporary shift from governments to corporations in relation to the protection and promotion of human rights, and reviews the evolving business and human rights policy agenda at the UN.

3.1   *The Ideology of Human Rights and the Responsibility of the State*

Much of the discourse of business and human rights arises from the UN's *Universal Declaration on Human Rights* (UDHR). UDHR, ratified in 1948, represented the first international attempt to constitute the notion of human rights. Amnesty International provides a conventional definition of human rights:

> Human rights are those rights that people have as a consequence of being human. They do not need to be given, bought, earned or inherited. Human rights are those basic standards without which people cannot live in dignity. (Amnesty International, 2005, p. 9)

The global significance of these ideas is captured by Howen (2005), who observed that the discourse of human rights has become *the* generally accepted normative standard for the way human beings should be treated.

Regardless of how compelling the idea that individuals should be entitled to basic standards for a dignified life might be, human rights are nevertheless a relatively modern, socially constructed,[6] and ideologically contested ideal (see OIC, 1990; Dembour, 2006). Similarly, some deep green environmentalists contend that the anthropocentrism at the core of the human rights agenda may be partially responsible for the precarious state of our planetary ecosystem (Vischer, 2005). At the outset of any discussion of business and human rights, it is therefore important to stress that human rights are political and ideological constructs as well as legal and physiological ones (Douzinas, 2000). The business and human rights debate needs to be cast as part of the broader, evolving (political) struggle for the meaning of all rights. Having said this, recognizing the socially constructed nature of rights does not preclude a decision to become involved in the struggle over their meaning based on a belief that they can be a force for good (McPhail, 2001b; Dembour, 2006).

Two treaties codified UDHR into international law in 1966: the International Covenant on Civil and Political Rights (ICCPR) and the International Covenant on Economic, Social and Cultural Rights (ICESCR). These treaties are collectively known as the International Bill of Rights. Although UDHR calls on every individual and every organ of society to play a role in realizing human rights, the International Bill of Rights requires nation states, not companies, to ratify conventions, protocols, and other human rights instruments. Historically, nation states have been held accountable for compliance with human rights treaties, including respecting the efforts of individuals to realize their rights. Within this legal framework, nation states have a duty not only to respect individual human rights (in the negative sense of not infringing), but also have an obligation to protect and fulfill these rights. Protecting human rights involves establishing mechanisms for redress when individuals feel that their human rights have been violated and providing individuals with the means to realize their rights where they are unable to do so themselves (Amnesty International, 2005).

Apart from some specific obligations under international criminal and humanitarian law, there are few binding legal responsibilities on corporations in relation to international human rights law (Ratner, 2001). However, the state's obligation to protect its citizens against human rights abuses by third parties includes abuses perpetrated by corporations. This requires states to put laws in place to ensure that their corporations do not violate internationally accepted human rights conventions. States normally do so through the implementation of domestic laws, although there are concerns over the willingness of some states to enforce such obligations (IBLF, 2005). While many corporations are subject to domestic human rights laws, there is growing concern over a state's ability to regulate MNCs for human rights abuses perpetrated outside of the jurisdictions within which they are domiciled (Amnesty International, 2005).

Scholars have become increasingly critical of a conceptualization of human rights that construes the state as the sole duty holder in both protecting and promoting human rights (Ratner, 2001). Ratner (2001, p. 461) argues for the 'need to view corporations, and not simply those working for them, as duty holders', a claim presumably made to increase the legal pressure on corporations to take their human rights obligations seriously.[7] There is a growing body of legal work[8] that demonstrates business complicity in human rights abuses across international jurisdictions (Oxford Pro Bono, 2008). There also has been significant progress in the individual's ability to seek redress from corporations for human rights abuses through class action law suits under alien tort (Amnesty International, 2006; Oxford Pro Bono, 2008).

The discourse on rights is intrinsically related to the construction of relationships and associated responsibilities between entities. While traditionally this relationship has been between individuals and states, the emerging business and human rights discourse reconstitutes this relationship as being amongst individuals, states, and corporations. It is important to re-stress the contentious nature of all of the above relationships.

Recent debates surrounding the detention of suspected terrorists in the US or illegal immigrants in Australia highlight the problematic ways in which governments reconstitute the notion of rights for political ends (Douzinas, 2000, 2007). Similarly, The *Kasky v. Nike* case has shown how corporations appropriate rights for their own ends, in this instance the right to free speech (Hess and Dunfee, 2007; Mayer, 2007). The potential conflicts between the interests of corporations and the human rights agenda questions how far multi-national corporations can and should be viewed as vehicles for promoting the realization of human rights. Amnesty International (2005) sought to extend corporate responsibility beyond compliance with the law to a broader moral responsibility for realizing rights. They stated that:

> one could argue that a corporation has a degree of (moral) responsibility towards society that goes beyond respecting and protecting human rights. For instance, when a company operates in a territory where the state is unable to fulfill the rights of its people, a company could be asked to act in order to ensure that individuals have access to those resources needed for survival. (Amnesty International, 2005, pp. 11–12)

Amnesty International (2005, p. 4) also advocated a positive role for corporations in promoting human rights in conflict and post-conflict zones:

> In such situations companies could try and reduce ethnic tensions and minimize prejudices among groups by promoting an atmosphere within the companies' direct sphere of influence that could contribute to normalising social relations in the community where the company operates.

Muchlinski (2001, p. 42) argued that corporate human rights obligations 'go beyond the furthest limits of responsibility hitherto imposed by human rights law in response to violations committed by private actors' and raised a number of questions about extending the scope of corporate accountability and responsibility for human rights. This included the extent to which corporations are reflexively constituted as they render an account for any human rights obligations. Muchlinski (2001, p. 44) commented that placing a responsibility on business to realize human rights 'appears to treat corporations as quasi-governmental public institutions. That is to give them a constitutional status that they neither deserve nor need'. It also fails to recognize the political nature of the rights–obligation structure of existing market relationships (Chang, 2002).

3.2 *The Rationale for the Shift in Focus from States to Corporations*

The growing focus on corporate accountability and human rights reflects the historical shift in global politics associated with the evolution of global capitalism. The rationale for the increased focus on human rights is in part related to the increased power of MNCs along with their increasingly complex relationships with nation states.

The shift of responsibility from nation states to corporations is predicated on the significant increase in the nature and volume of investments by MNCs in developing countries and their power in comparison to the states in which they are investing.[9] As noted above, almost half of the largest 100 economies in the world are corporations (Korten, 2001; Rugman, 2005). Their investments in developing countries are often couched within the terms of bilateral investment treaties and mediated by stabilization clauses that can create a tension between protecting the corporations' investments and the protection and fulfillment of human rights obligations. These investments are often partially funded by home states via national Export Credit Agencies, which could compromise the home state's ability to ensure that all human rights obligations are met by the MNCs. As the power of corporations has increased, they have simultaneously become more independent of state oversight. Ratner (2001, p. 463) commented:

> Many of the largest TNEs [transnational enterprises] have headquarters in one state, share-holders in others and operations worldwide. If the host state fails to regulate the acts of the company, other states, including the state of the corporation's nationality, may well choose to abstain from regulation based on the extraterritorial nature of the acts at issue.

The International Business Leaders Initiative on Human Rights (IBLF, 2005), for example, concluded that:

> The rights of transnational firms – their ability to operate and expand globally – have increased greatly over the past generation as a result of trade agreements, bilateral investment treaties and domestic liberalisation [...] In light of this transformation in the institutional features of the world economy, it is hardly surprising that the transnational corporate sector – and by extension the entire universe of business – has attracted increased attention by other social actors, including civil society and States themselves. (IBLF, 2005, p. 12)

The shift of human rights responsibilities from nation states to MNCs is largely motivated by a perceived gap in global governance, resulting from the global neo-liberal promotion of free market economics. The human rights regulatory response also reflects a neo-liberal ideology that ostensibly seeks to reduce the size of the state and make social institutions and private actors responsible through market modes of governance (Chang, 2002). So, while the neo-liberal free market ideology is identified as a source of the problem (to the extent that it results in large MNCs), the same ideology constructs the solution in terms of increased roles for markets and private actors. These contradictions require much more critical analysis within accounting education than they have received to date.

3.3 *The Evolving Regulatory Environment*

The re-positioning of the regulatory function of states and the private sector has been at the heart of UN policy development for the past two decades. In a speech to the World Economic Forum, in 1998, then UN General Secretary Kofi Annan commented (quoted in Zammit, 2003, p. 31):

> A fundamental shift has occurred. The United Nations once dealt with governments. By now we know that peace and prosperity cannot be achieved without active partnerships involving governments, international organizations, the business community and civil society. In today's world we depend on each other. The business of the United Nations involves the business of the world.

Under Annan's leadership, the UN attempted to change its relationship with business. This policy shift was reflected in the launch of the Global Compact in 1999 at the Davos World Economic Forum (Nolan, 2010). The Global Compact was designed to be a forum for the development of a global learning network rather than a regulatory instrument. Membership was conditional on a letter to the UN Secretary General indicating support for the Global Compact principles.

In 2003 the UN outlined the human rights duties for companies in *The United Nations Norms on Responsibilities of Transnational Corporations and Other Business Enterprises with Regard to Human Rights*. The norms represented an attempt to clearly define the human rights responsibilities of corporations. The Global Compact had been criticized for its voluntary nature and lack of enforcement, with many pointing to the lack of evidence that it was producing substantive organizational change (Nolan, 2010). The UN norms represented a further refinement of business responsibility for human rights in contrast to the broad principles of the Global Compact (Nolan, 2010).

The Business Leaders Initiative on Human Rights (BLIHR) was established in 2003 in an attempt to show how UDHR could be translated into business policy and practice.[10] BLIHR (2010) explained that:

> By 2003, the subject of business and human rights was receiving greater international attention with the development of the United Nations Global Compact and the growing momentum within the context of the UN Sub-Commission on Human Rights where the so-called 'Norms' on Business and Human Rights were being proposed. BLIHR agreed to take an agnostic position on the Norms during their development, when most business associations were stridently opposed and to 'roadtest' the content of the Sub-Commission adopted Norms in business contexts with the aim of developing an evidence-based response. (BLIHR, 2010, p. 8)

The BLIHR represents just one of a number of human rights initiatives from within the business community. Some businesses were actively opposed to the UN norms[11] and no doubt some of these initiatives were motivated in order to mitigate the prospect of greater regulation and reshape the meaning and practice of human rights in the interests of corporations. The BLIHR and other initiatives represent powerful (though not necessarily strategic) interventions in the development of business responsibilities for human rights.

In 2005, partially in response to the impasse generated by the UN norms (Nolan, 2010), the UN appointed Professor John Ruggie of Harvard as a Special Representative of the UN Secretary-General on Business and Human Rights, with the mandate to 'identify and clarify standards of corporate responsibility and accountability for transnational corporations and other business enterprises with regard to human rights' (United Nations Human Rights, Office of the High Commissioner for Human Rights, n.d.). Nolan (2010; see also Taylor, 2011) contended that the appointment was promoted by an urgency to navigate a way between the apparently ineffectual voluntarism of the Global Compact and the failed attempt to develop regulation at the international level through the UN norms. Ruggie[12] was specifically tasked to:

> elaborate on the role of states in effectively regulating the role of businesses, including through international cooperation; to research and clarify concepts such as "complicity" and "sphere of influence"; to develop materials and methodologies for undertaking human rights impact assessments of business activities; and to compile a compendium of best practices of states and businesses. (Amnesty International, 2005, pp. 10–11)

In 2008, Professor Ruggie presented a policy framework of three core principles to the UN Human Rights Council to guide the business and human rights agenda. These principles were:

- the state's duty to protect against human rights abuses by third parties, including business;
- businesses' responsibility to respect human rights; and
- the need for more effective access to remedies for victims of human rights abuses.

In June 2008, the United Nations' Human Rights Council explicitly stated that corporations have a responsibility to respect human rights. Subsequently, Professor Ruggie developed a series of Guiding Principles on Business and Human Rights designed to implement the Protect, Respect, Remedy policy framework. These guiding principles were formally ratified by the UN Human Rights Council in June 2011, an event widely regarded as being one of the most significant developments in corporate governance in a decade (Taylor, 2011).

In presenting the Protect, Respect, Remedy policy framework to the UN in 2010, Ruggie announced: 'The era of declaratory CSR is over' (quoted in Taylor 2011, p. 10). Ruggie (2010, quoted in Taylor, 2011, p. 10) commented that 'the corporate responsibility to respect human rights cannot be met by words alone: it requires specific measures by means of which companies can know and show that they respect rights'. Taylor (2011, p. 21) explained the regulatory model underpinning the three foundation principles as follows:

> The Guiding Principles establish a theory of regulation in which the general duty to regulate falls under the first pillar of the Framework (the state duty to protect human rights), the specific theory of attribution to business entities is set out under the second pillar (the business reponsibility to respect human rights), and the issue of business liability is dealt with under the third pillar on remedies.

The principles purportedly represent an attempt to move beyond the lack of conceptual clarity and corporate accountability of the Global Compact towards more binding corporate responsibility for human rights (Nolan, 2010; Taylor, 2011).[13,14]

The Protect, Respect, Remedy framework and the Guiding Principles are therefore significant in that they represent a new governance regime in business and human rights (Backer, 2011; Taylor, 2011). The significance of the framework and principles lies, firstly, in its attempt to develop a specific definition of business responsibility for human rights from their business activities and relationships[15] and, secondly, in its identification of due diligence for human rights risk as the key method by which this responsibility should be operationalized (Taylor, 2011). Both developments have direct implications for accounting in relation to models of corporate accountability and accounting processes and practices. Commenting on the responsibilities of the state in relation to outsourcing their service delivery, Ruggie (2011, p. 10, emphasis added) argued that: 'States should ensure that they can effectively oversee the enterprise's activities [. . .] through the provision of *adequate independent monitoring and accountability mechanisms*'.

The policy and regulatory environment in relation to corporate responsibility for human rights has evolved significantly over the past two decades (Nolan, 2010).[16] The most recent development in the form of the Guiding Principles is significant for a number of reasons, not least because of the impact that the focus on business activities and human rights due diligence may have on both internal accounting systems and external corporate disclosure.

4. Human Rights and the Business Practice Environment.

This section explores how the human rights policy agenda outlined above is being translated into the business practice environment and how this agenda is impinging on business practices (Cooper, Coulson and Taylor, 2011). These impacts include, but are not limited to, access to capital; reputation risk; legal risk; a plethora of voluntary codes; along with other regulatory mechanisms like the Organisation for Economic Co-operation and Development's (OECD) National Contact Points.

Human rights are now part of MNCs' operational world. Pressure on corporate performance in relation to human rights is emerging from a number of different sources, primarily access to consumer markets, access to capital and reputational risk. The child labor controversies of companies like Reebok, Nike and Gap and the connection between Shell's operations in Nigeria and the execution of Ken Saro-Wiwa during the 1990s have brought human rights into the spotlight of those concerned with managing supply chains and corporate reputational risk (BLIHR, 2010).

Human rights-related issues are also impinging on the debt financing of foreign direct investment (FDI) through banks. Cases of bad publicity arising from allegations of 'dirty loans' may be behind the increasing use of human rights impact assessments by banks when evaluating debt finance requests from clients (Amnesty International, 2006). Human rights are also becoming increasingly important in decision making processes in relation to government export subsidies through export credit agencies and access to equity through ethical investment funds and sovereign wealth funds. The exclusion of Wal-Mart because of its poor human rights record from the Norwegian state pension fund illustrates the possible sanctions arising from human rights breaches. Greater scrutiny is being directed at the connection between the use of government funds and corporations' human rights record.

In addition to the UN Global Compact[17] a number of other voluntary international standards now explicitly delineate business responsibilities in relation to respecting human rights, such as the International Labour Organization's Tripartite Declaration, which outlines a number of workplace human rights. Governments are also embarking on initiatives to encourage companies to address human rights. In 2000, the US and UK governments, seven major oil and mining companies, along with nine international NGOs, publicly expressed their support for the Voluntary Principles on Security and Human Rights. These principles were drawn up over a year-long dialogue convened by the US State Department and the UK Foreign Office. Since then the Norwegian and Dutch governments have joined the process, and 16 companies were participating as of December 2005. Along with these government initiatives there are also a raft of sector-specific principles (see Table 1).

In 1976, the OECD produced its Guidelines for Multinational Enterprises, which contained the principles and standards to be followed for the purpose of achieving sustainable development. While the principles are voluntary, countries were required to establish National Contact Points (NCPs) as a mechanism whereby concerns over violation of the guidelines could be reported.[18] These NCPs provide avenues to pursue allegations of human rights abuses. The Royal Bank of Scotland (RBS) (now predominantly state owned) was reported via the UK NCP in relation to loans provided to Vedanta Plc due

Table 1. Sector specific initiatives incorporating human rights.

Extractive industries	Retail	Finance	Electronics
• Voluntary Principles on Security and Human Rights	• Ethical Trading Initiative	• Equator Principles	• Electronic Industry Code of Conduct
• Extractive Industries Transparency Initiative	• Fair Labor Association	• United Nations Environment Programme Finance Initiative Human Rights Toolkit	• Global e-Sustainability Initiative
• Kimberley Process	• Clean Clothes Campaign		
• Communities and Small-Scale Mining	• SA8000		

Adapted from Oxford Pro Bono (2008).

to the company's disregard for the rights of indigenous people in the Indian state of Orissa.[19] Kevin Smith from the NGO *Platform* commented: 'The Treasury has a legal duty to ensure that RBS isn't using taxpayers' money to support companies that trample over human rights and trash the climate' (Macalister, 2009). The language of human rights and the policy discussion outlined in Section 3 can be seen to impinge on the business environment in a number of ways.

The BLIHR concluded that: 'the corporate responsibility to respect human rights has become the baseline expectation for business behavior – in particular through the application of human rights due diligence' (BLIHR, 2010, p. 8). The language of human rights seems to be a crucial factor in maintaining corporations' social license to operate and securing legitimacy with a broad range of stakeholders. According to a 2006 survey of Fortune Global 500 companies, nine out of 10 corporate respondents had human rights principles in place. More than half of the FTSE 100 companies had adopted a human rights policy and over 60% of respondents referenced UDHR within these policies.

The objective of this section was to outline examples of business and human right practices that require further critical analysis as to whether participation in the development of voluntary human rights codes is strategic self-interest or a form of due diligence undertaken to access funds. The UN Guiding Principles explicitly locates responsibility for human rights within the context of businesses' activities and clearly establishes a need for managers and accountants to be able to undertake processes of due diligence for human rights risks. These Guiding Principles raise a number of challenges for accounting educators, including how to critically explore the ways in which conventional accounting systems may make human rights violations less visible due to accountings' propensity to remove the human from human rights (McPhail, 2001b), and how human rights policy discourses are translated into everyday business practice in ways that paradoxically work against the interests of the individuals whose rights they are ostensibly designed to protect (Cooper, Coulson and Taylor, 2011).

5. Human Rights and Sustainability

Having outlined the evolution of business and human rights from their conceptual underpinnings to their impact on everyday business practice, this section explicitly engages with the complex relationships between human rights and sustainability in order to address how these two discourses have been construed as speaking to different sets of concerns. As Picolotti and Taillant (2003, p. XIV) comment, 'local and international organizations, governments and civil society tend to isolate human rights issues into a limited sphere and treat environmental degradation as an entirely unrelated issue'. This section has two objectives: firstly, to show how notions of human rights and sustainability are linked together within the business practice environment; and, secondly, to briefly discuss the synergies and conflicts between these two contemporary discourses.

As commented above, the UN clearly links the state of the environment with the realization of human rights. Principle 1 of the 1972 Stockholm Conference on the Human Environment states that:

> Man has the fundamental right to freedom, equality and adequate conditions of life, in an environment of a quality that permits a life of dignity and well-being, and he bears a solemn responsibility to protect and improve the environment for present and future generations.

It is unsurprising that human rights and sustainability are recurring themes in international developments such as the Global Compact and the Global Reporting Initiative (GRI), which bring together issues of human rights, labor rights, the environment, and anti-corruption. Perhaps as a consequence of this, human rights issues are often disclosed under the umbrella of sustainability within the corporate social responsibility media of corporations. Xstrata's 2009 sustainability report, for example, contains extensive reference to human rights and referred to a combined sustainability and human rights framework in operation in the company. It stated that:

> Our unique Sustainable Development (SD) Framework guides Xstrata's commodity businesses and provides assurance for the Board that standards are being upheld. It addresses all SD-related topics and is backed by a detailed set of SD Performance Standards. Our SD Framework is aligned with international standards including the International Council on Mining and Minerals principles and guidelines, the Precautionary Principle, the UN Global Compact, Voluntary Principles on Security and Human Rights, ISO 31000, ISO 14001 and OHSAS 18001. (Xstrata, 2009, p. 24)

While Xstrata's primary concerns with human rights seem to relate to security and labor issues, there is evidence of an emerging connection amongst human rights, environmental rights, and sustainability issues, for example:

> The primary human rights issues in our business relate to:
>
> *Labour:* The rights of our employees and contractors to work for equal pay, associate freely, to a safe and healthy workplace, to non-discrimination and to their legal rights;
>
> *Security:* The conduct of security organisations protecting our operations at certain specific locations where there is a threat to our people or assets. The conduct of public security forces who enter our sites during the execution of their duties; and
>
> *Communities:* The impact our operations may have on communities includes the use of land and mineral assets, economic impacts, displacement, *access to resources such as water and energy and other environmental impacts.* In certain circumstances disagreements over these factors can lead to an environment in which human rights are compromised. (Xstrata, 2009, p. 32, emphasis added)

The reference to access to resources such as water and energy may be reflective of emergent discussions within the rights arena that explicitly construe the right to water as a human right (Alvarez, 2003).[20] Alvarez (2003, p. 72) commented that: 'The right to water is understood as part of the right to life, as a component of the right to health and as part of the right'. Bradbrook and Gardam (2006) similarly discuss the advantages of construing access to energy as a human right. It would seem clear that a critical understanding of human rights needs to address the emergent links between human rights and sustainability. Vischer (2005, p. 47, see also Shelton, 1991) asked:

> How do human rights and sustainability relate to one another? There has been a growing awareness that there are limits to human development on our planet. More and more people have to live with the limited resources offered by nature. The quality of life of future generations is threatened. What does this imply for human rights? This is being heatedly debated.

The articulation of human rights and sustainability issue is being debated, but not in the accounting literature,[21] in accounting departments, or business schools. Similarly, future business professionals or accountants are not being exposed to this debate in their professional education.

Nearly 20 years ago the UN placed the inter-relationship between environmental protection and human rights to the fore of international policy debates (Shelton, 1991).

Principle 1 of the Stockholm Declaration on the Human Environment was subsequently reinforced by Principle 10 of the 1992 Rio Declaration on Environment and Development, and the Aarhus Convention (1999) secured a landmark agreement on citizens' rights to the environment. The Convention stated that:

> In order to contribute to the protection of the right of every person present and future generations to live in an environment adequate to his or her health and well-being, each party shall guarantee the rights of access to information, public participation in decision making, and access to justice in environmental matters in accordance with the provisions of this Convention. (UNECE, 1999, Article 1)

The significance of the Aarhus Convention lies in how it articulated the rights to environment, information, and participation in matters that have an impact on the environment. Another illustration of this articulation can be observed in the 1981 African Charter on Human and Peoples' Rights, which was the first human rights treaty to expressly recognize the right of all peoples 'to a generally satisfactory environment favorable to their development' (Shelton, 1991, p. 125).[22]

While the link between human rights and sustainability has been articulated in a number of conventions and treaties, the exact nature of the relationship is debated. Firstly, the environment could be viewed as being inextricably related to the enjoyment of basic human rights. In this instance, rights may be violated as a result of environmental damage (Shelton, 1991).[23] Shelton (1991) explained that the rights threatened by environmental degradation include: the right to life; the right to health; the right to suitable working conditions; the right to information (for example, in relation to the dumping of toxic substance); the right to an adequate standard of living; and the right to political participation. Here the environment was seen to be a prerequisite to the enjoyment of fundamental rights. However, there is a danger that prioritizing the environment can be used to stop the enjoyment of other rights.[24] Hamm (2001) elaborated on the tension between sustainability and rights by contrasting the right to a healthy environment with the emerging discussion around the idea of the right to development.[25] Hamm (2001) observed that this tension was related to the debate on whether the right to development should be limited by the need for sustainability. Hamm (2001, p. 7, see also Udombana, 2000; Meier and Fox, 2008) further commented on how the Human Development Report 2000 combined an 'understanding of sustainable human development, embracing the economic, political, social, environmental, and cultural dimensions of development'.

Alternatively, it can be argued that the environment needs to be preserved for its own sake. This view is articulated in terms of the rights of the environment. A third perspective views the environment and human rights as partially overlapping, but that not every human right has an environmental impact (Shelton, 1991). This third approach identifies areas of alignment and conflict between the two agendas.

Some commentators suggest that integrating human rights with the sustainability agenda may be advantageous for a number of reasons. Firstly, a case is made for viewing the link between human rights and sustainability in pragmatic terms (Philip, 2005). This perspective argues that the sustainability agenda can be pursued by building upon existing legal obligations related to human rights treaties and by using existing national human rights institutions (Philip, 2005). Bradbrook and Gardam (2006) explained the benefits of linking the sustainability agenda with existing human rights frameworks to impose social and environmental obligations on nation states. It was also contended that the human rights discourse, specifically on civil and political rights, provided both clarity and credibility to an often vague set of environmental commitments to participation and empowerment. Bradbrook and Gardam (2006, p. 414), in their discussion of access to energy as a right, explained that: 'the debate over energy has been somewhat random and uncoordinated. The human rights framework may provide a mechanism for addressing this deficiency'.

Over and above this pragmatic strategy, a second approach seeks to develop a set of specific environmental rights. Shelton (1991) explained that these may be construed in terms of rights *of* the environment as well as rights *to* the environment. Environmental rights can be taken to mean rights that the environment possesses, as opposed to rights that humans have to a sustainable environment. This view is particularly challenging for developing countries. Shelton (1991) suggested that the development of a specific 'right to environment' has gained some international momentum and may be the predominant emerging view. Interestingly, these environmental rights were related to existing democratic rights to involvement in the political process and the right to information.

Agyeman, Bullard and Evans (2002, see also Meier and Fox, 2008; Adams *et al.*, 2011) provided a more nuanced political economy discussion of the link between human equality and sustainability.[26] Aygeman (2001) identified that environmental degradation (although construed as a global problem) tends to have a greater impact on the poor and argued that there was an empirical link amongst income distribution, civil rights, political rights, and the quality of the environment. Drawing on Adeola (2000), he contended that much of the environmental degradation caused by MNCs represented a major human rights violation against local people caught in the path of globalization, and that one of the best ways to protect the environment was to ensure civil and political rights. Agyeman, Bullard and Evans (2002, p. 77) commented that 'wherever in the world environmental degradation is happening, they are almost always linked to questions of social justice, equity, rights and people's quality of life in the widest sense'. They drew on Lipietz (1996) to argue for the recognition of *human environmental* rights. Agyeman, Bullard and Evans (2002, p. 83) commented on how the success of the environmental movement was linked to the extent to which it was able to 'tap into the discourse and rhetoric of the civil rights movement'. Indeed, they contend that the effectiveness of the environmental movement was related to the extent to which environmental justice was linked to a labor and social justice master frame.[27] Agyeman, Bullard and Evans (2002, p. 78) concluded that a 'truly sustainable society is one where wider questions of social needs and welfare, and economic opportunity are integrally related to environmental limits imposed by supporting ecosystems'.

There is a substantial body of literature that seeks to connect and problematize human rights and sustainability. Vischer (2005, p. 48) concluded that:

> Some people believe that a new "generation" of human rights is called for and that the catalogue of rights should be extended to the natural world, expressly stating that all human beings have a right to a healthy environment. But is this a realistic proposition? Can the two concepts of human rights and sustainability be so easily combined? The two concepts have different roots and serve different purposes. The Universal Declaration of Human Rights is intended to create a social and political order guaranteeing the development of every individual human person and of humanity as a whole. Starting with the rights of the individual, it sets out the basic prerequisites for a just social order. It is not immediately concerned with preserving the planet. The concept of sustainability has developed out of the disturbing awareness that human activity has sparked off an inexorable process of destruction. The Universal Declaration of Human Rights is essentially more anthropocentric. [...]. How can these two objectives be brought into line with one another?

The question of how the two discourses of human rights and sustainability come together, practically, in terms of what corporations are doing and reporting, and theoretically, is of critical importance to any attempt to incorporate human rights into accounting and business curricula.

6. Conclusion

The human rights responsibilities of corporations are emerging as an issue of considerable importance, which is inextricably linked to the pursuit of sustainability. However, as yet human rights have failed to make their way into the curricula of business schools, accounting departments, accounting institutes, or corporate social responsibility discourses. This paper explored how the discourse and apparatus of international human rights is shifting to focus attention on the responsibilities of corporations in relation to the protection and promotion of human rights and how these rights are construed in relation to sustainability. The paper presented an argument for incorporating human rights into sustainability education, which is currently more prevalent within the business and accounting curriculum and has offered some tentative initial suggestions as to what a business and accounting education for human rights might involve. While the outline curriculum is tentative, the need to critically engage students with the broader political economic function of accounting is imperative. The business and human rights discourse provides another opportunity to do this. As Sikka (2011, p. 827) commented:

> A focus on human rights can reinvigorate accounting, corporate governance and CSR research and can help to strengthen democracy, public accountability and provide a better world.

While education does play an obvious role in the realization of both human rights and sustainable development, it would be naïve to think that education on its own will stop business complicity in human rights abuses. Of course, human rights need to be incorporated into the business school curriculum, but at the same time it has incorporated into international standards governing foreign direct investment; the protocols guiding government subsidy though Export Credit Agencies; the ethical screening practices of investment funds; new accountability practices; and the conditions of bilateral trade agreements (Amnesty International, 2006). As academics we can research and lobby for change in these areas, but perhaps we have an immediate and more local opportunity to start with what we teach.

Notes

[1]Human Rights Watch (2005) claimed AngloGold Ashanti made payments to a 'murderous armed group' in the Democratic Republic of Congo (DRC) to gain access to DRC's natural resources. An expert report to the UN Security Council in January 2007 reported a clear link between the activities of armed militia and the exploitation of the DRC's natural resources.

[2]The accounting literature does contain some research on human rights, although not always labelled as such. Adams and McPhail (2004) provide an analysis of corporate engagement with discrimination. However, a discussion that seeks to frame corporate social responsibility in terms of the Universal Declaration of Human Rights is substantively missing.

[3]See *Critical Perspectives on Accounting* (Volume 22, Issue 8) for an attempt to systematically engage accounting research with the emerging human rights discourse.

[4]These include but are not limited to: the ideology of the autonomous, dignified individual, the pragmatist engagement with corporations, and the neo-liberal belief in markets.

[5]The Tax Justice Network, along with 80 other NGOs, called for greater transparency in the reporting of turnover, profit, and tax by country, based on figures that suggest that tax dodging costs developing economies $160 billion a year, which is greater than they receive in aid (e.g. see Christian Aid, 2009).

[6]As Douzinas (2000, p. 7) explains: 'The prime function of human rights is to construct the individual person as a subject (of law)'.

[7]See also Muchlinski (2001).

[8]See also the work by International Commission of Jurists at www.icj.org

[9]The International Council on Mining and Minerals (ICMM), a body set up to champion the mining sector's interests, commented that: 'One example is the current lack of clarity over the boundaries between companies and states in upholding human rights while seeking to uphold human rights within their legitimate

"sphere of influence", for example, companies also clearly need to avoid becoming political actors, or interfere in the political affairs of host countries' (International Council on Mining and Minerals, 2006, p. 4). This comment seems naïve and ignores the obvious point that companies are political actors and do have an impact on the affairs of host countries.

[10]The BLIHR brought together a group of 10 major companies with the aim of embedding human rights more firmly within corporate consciousness. BLIHR's objective was to indicate how international human rights standards could be applied in the context of business policy and practice. The BLIHR was superseded in March 2009 by the Global Business Initiative on Human Rights, which focuses on the application of human rights to business practice in emerging economies (BLIHR, 2010, p. 8). This new body engaged with a further question: 'how do human rights contribute to the way a business might understand its (mainly moral) responsibilities to the broader international development agenda?' (BLIHR, 2010, p. 8).

[11]The UN Norms were never adopted by the Commission on Human Rights, although they were not rejected either.

[12]'Human rights and transnational corporations and other business enterprises', UN Commission on Human Rights, Resolution 2005/69, adopted 20 April 2005, para 1(a).

[13]Nolan (2010, p. 16) commented that 'the principles cited in the Global Compact do not constitute a sufficient basis for designing enforceable standards and are beneficial more from the point of view of acting as yet another indicator in the global arena of the general relevance of international human rights norms to business [...]. Along with the lack of specificity in defining the relevant rights, is a vagueness concerning the scope of the initiative, in particular the degree of responsibility a company assumes in embracing, supporting and enacting these rights'.

[14]Some NGOs felt that the language didn't go far enough in specifying governmental and corporate responsibility for violations.

[15]Grounding business responsibility in terms of activities and relationships clarifies the amorphous notion of 'sphere of influence' (Taylor, 2011).

[16]Responsibility for overseeing the development and application of the Guiding Principles has not been located within the Global Compact, which may be reflective of sentiments regarding the Global Compact's lack of legitimacy.

[17]The Compact now has around 4000 business members from all corners of the world, although another 70,000 TNEs and countless millions of small and medium-sized enterprises are not yet parties to the Global Compact Principles (Oxford Pro Bono, 2008).

[18]NCPs report to the OECD Committee on International Investment and Multinational Enterprises (CIME) on an annual basis.

[19]The company proposed to build an opencast bauxite mine near the holy site of Niyamgiri.

[20]The UN has now ratified a right to water and sanitation (UN Resolution A/HRC/15/L.14).

[21]Adams et al. (2011) are critical of the separation of the MDG of sustainability and poverty reduction goals implicit within the Millennium Development Goals. They contend that there is a clear need for strategies to alleviate poverty and sustainability strategies to be aligned.

[22]The OECD articulated a need to construe a 'decent' environment as a human right, a point to which the International Labour Organization also alluded (Shelton, 1991). The right to a healthy environment is contained within the Bill of Rights of the South African constitution (Tilbury et al., 2002).

[23]While all environmental degradation does have an impact on the enjoyment of rights, it can also promote other rights, or the rights of others.

[24]This can often happen in relation to economic development, where a right to development is prioritized over other civil and political rights.

[25]There are questions as to whether the right to development is a right in its own or is constructed from other human rights.

[26]Agyeman, Bullard and Evans (2002) present the inclusion of the human rights into the environmental and sustainability agenda as a challenge to the sustainability agenda's focus on biodiversity.

[27]Indeed, Taylor (2000) links the success of environmentalism with its links to the civil rights movement.

References

Adams, C. A. and McPhail, K. J. (2004) Reporting and the politics of difference: (non) disclosure on ethnic minorities, *Abacus*, 40(3), pp. 405–435.

Adams, C. A., Heijltjes, M. H., Jack, G., Marjoribanks, T. and Powell, M. (2011) The development of leaders able to respond to climate change and sustainability challenges: the role of business schools, *Sustainability Accounting, Management and Policy Journal*, 2(1) pp. 165–171.

Adeola, F. O. (2000) Cross-national environmental justice and human rights issues: a review of evidence in the developing world, *American Behavioral Scientist*, 43, pp. 686–706.

Agyeman, J. (2001) Ethnic minorities in Britain: short change, systematic indifference and sustainable development, *Journal of Environmental Policy and Planning*, 3(1), pp. 15–30.

Agyeman, J., Bullard, R. and Evans, B. (2002) Exploring the nexus: bringing together sustainability, *Environmental Justice and Equity Space and Polity*, 6(1), pp. 77–90.

Alvarez, I. (2003) The right to water as a human right, in: R.P. Picolotti and J. D. Taillant (Eds) *Linking Human Rights and the Environment*, pp. 71–82 (Arizona, US: University Press of Arizona).

Amnesty International (2005) *Human Rights and Business Pages. Non-Discrimination and Equality* (London, UK: Amnesty International).

Amnesty International (2006) *Human Rights, Trade and Investment Matters* (London: Amnesty International).

Arrington, C. E. and Francis, J. R. (1993) Accounting as a human practice: the appeal of other voices, *Accounting, Organizations and Society*, 18(2–3), pp. 105–106.

Aronowitz, S. and Giroux, H. A. (1991) *Postmodern Education Politics, Culture And Social Criticism* (Minneapolis: University of Minnesota).

Backer, L. C. (2011) From institutional misalignment to socially sustainable governance: the guiding principles for the implementation of the United Nations' 'Protect, Respect and Remedy' and the construction of inter systemic global governance, *Pacific McGregor Global Business & Development Law Journal*, pp. 102–216.

Bradbrook, A. J. and Gardam, J. G. (2006) Placing access to energy services within a human rights framework, *Human Rights Quarterly*, 28(2), pp. 389–415.

Business Leaders Initiative on Human Rights (2004) *Report 2: Work in Progress* (London: BLIHR).

Business Leaders Initiative on Human Rights (2010) *The Millennium Development Goals and Human Rights: Companies Taking a Rights-aware Approach to Development*. Available at http://www.ihrb.org/pdf/BLIHR_Human_Rights_and_MDGs.pdf

Chang, H. (2002) Breaking the mould – an institutionalist political economy alternative to the neo-liberal theory of the market and the state, *Cambridge Journal of Economics*, 26(5), pp. 539–559.

Christian Aid (2005) *Flagship of Failure: The Implementation of the OECD Guidelines and Approach to Corporate Accountability with Amnesty International & Friends of the Earth* (London: Christian Aid).

Christian Aid (2009) *False Profits. Robbing the Poor to Pay the Rich* (London: Christian Aid).

Clements, C. E., Neill, J. D. and Stovall, O. S. (2009) The impact of cultural differences on the convergence of international accounting codes of ethics, *Journal of Business Ethics*, 90(3), pp. 383–391.

Cooper, C., Coulson, A. and Taylor, P. (2011) Accounting for human rights: doxic health and safety practices – the accounting lesson from ICL, *Critical Perspectives on Accounting*, 22, pp. 738–758.

Dembour, M. B. (2006) *Who Believes in Human Rights: Reflections on the European Convention* (Cambridge: Cambridge University Press).

Dillard, J. F. (1991) Accounting as a critical social science, *Accounting Auditing And Accountability Journal*, 4(1), pp. 8–28.

Douzinas, C. (2000) *The End of Human Rights* (Oxford: Hart Publishing).

Douzinas, C. (2007) *Human Rights and Empire. The Political Philosophy of Cosmopolitanism* (New York: Routledge-Cavendish).

Entwistle, H. (1979) *Antonio Gramsci: Conservative Schooling For Radical Politics* (London, UK: Routledge & Kegan Paul).

Farrell, B. and Cobbin, D. (2000) A content analysis of codes of ethics from fifty-seven national accounting organizations, *Business Ethics: A European Review*, 9(3), pp. 180–190.

Fien, J. (ed.) (1993) *Environmental Education: A Pathway to Sustainability* (Victoria, Geelong: Deakin University Press).

Gallhofer, S. and Haslam, J. (1996) Analysis of Bentham's Chestomathia, or towards a critique of accounting education, *Critical Perspectives On Accounting*, 7, pp. 13–31.

Giroux, H. A. (1983) *Theory and Resistance in Education: A Pedagogy for the Opposition* (Massachusetts, USA: Bergin & Garvey).

Gray, R. H., Bebbington, J. and McPhail, K. (1994) Teaching ethics and the ethics of teaching: educating for immorality and a possible case for social and environmental accounting, *Accounting Education: An International Journal*, 3(1), pp. 51–75.

Hamm, B. I. (2001) A human rights approach to development, *Human Rights Quarterly*, 23(4), pp. 1005–1031.

Hess, D. and Dunfee, T. (2007) The Kasky-Nike threat to corporate social reporting. Implementing a standard of optimum truth disclosure as a solution, *Business Ethics Quarterly*, 17(1), pp. 5–32.

Howen, N. (2005) Business, human rights and accountability, speech delivered at the Business and Human Rights Conference organised by the Danish Section of the International Commission of Jurists, Copenhagen, 21 September.

Human Rights Watch (2005) *The Curse of Gold* (New York: Human Rights Watch).

IBLF (2005) Human Rights. It's your business. The case for corporate engagement, International Business Leaders Forum. Available at www.iblf.org/humanrights/

International Council on Mining and Minerals (2006) *Submission to UN Secretary General's Special Representative on Human Rights and Business* (London: ICMM). (London: ICMM).

Korten, D. C. (2001) *When Corporations Rule the World* (Bloomfield: Kumarian Press).

Lipietz, A. (1996) Geography, ecology, democracy, *Antipode*, 28, pp. 219–228.

Lewis, L., Humphrey, C. and Owen, D. (1992) Accounting and the social: a pedagogic perspective, *British Accounting Review*, 24(3), pp. 219–233.

Macalister, T. (2009) Treasury taken to court for RBS loans to Vedanta Resources, *Guardian*, 18 October. Available at http://www.theguardian.com/business/2009/oct/18/rbs-vedanta-loan-court-case

Macdonald, K. (2011) Re-thinking 'spheres of responsibility': business responsibility for indirect harm, *Journal of Business Ethics*, 99, pp. 549–563.

Mayer, D. (2007) *Kasky v. Nike* and the quarrelsome question of corporate free speech, *Business Ethics Quarterly*, 17(1), pp. 65–96.

McPhail, K. J. (2001a) The dialectic of accounting education: from role identity to ego identity, *Critical Perspectives on Accounting*, 12, pp. 471–500.

McPhail, K. J. (2001b) The other objective of ethics education: rehumanising the accounting profession: a study of ethics education in law, engineering, medicine and accountancy, *Journal of Business Ethics*, 34(3/4), pp. 279–298.

Meier, B. M. and Fox, A. M. (2008) Development as health: employing the collective right to development to achieve the goals of the individual right to health, *Human Rights Quarterly*, 30(2), pp. 259–355.

Muchlinski, P. (2001) Human rights and multinationals – is there a problem? *International Affairs*, 77, pp. 31–47.

Nolan, J. L. (2009) Corporate responsibility for economic, social and cultural rights: rights in search of a remedy? *Journal of Business Ethics*, 87, pp. 433–451.

Nolan, J. (2010) The United Nations compact with business: hindering or helping the protection of human rights?, University of New South Wales, Faculty of Law Research Series, Paper 10.

Non Governmental Liaison Service (NGLS) (2002) Roundup 90, May.

OIC (1990) *The Cairo Declaration on Human Rights in Islam* (Cairo, Egypt: Organisation of the Islamic Conference).

Oxford Pro Bono (2008) *Obstacles to Justice and Redress for Victims of Corporate Human Rights Abuse* (Oxford, UK: Oxford Pro Bono).

Philip, A. (2005) Ships passing in the night: the current state of the human rights and development debate seen through the lens of the millennium development goals, *Human Rights Quarterly*, 27(3), pp. 755–829.

Picolottie, R. P. and Taillant, J. D. (2003) *Linking Human Rights and the Environment* (Arizona, US: University Press of Arizona).

Poullaos, C. (2004) Globalisation, accounting critique and the university, *Critical Perspectives on Accounting*, 15(4–5), pp. 715–730.

Ratner, S. R. (2001) Corporations and human rights: a theory of legal responsibility, *The Yale Law Journal*, 111(3), pp. 443–545.

Ruggie, J. (2011) *Report of the Special Representative of the Secretary-General on the Issue of Human Rights and Transnational Corporations and other Business Enterprises* (Geneva: United Nations).

Rugman, A. (2005) *The Regional Multinationals* (Cambridge, UK: Cambridge University Press).

Schweiker, W. (1993) Accounting for ourselves: accounting practice and the discourse of ethics, *Accounting Organizations & Society*, 18(2/3), pp. 231–252.

Seppala, N (2009) Business and the international human rights regime: a comparison of UN initiatives, *Journal of Business Ethics*, 87, pp. 401–417.

Shearer, T. (2002) Ethics and accountability: from the for-itself to the for-the-other, *Accounting Organizations & Society*, 27, pp. 541–573.

Shelton, D. (1991) Human rights, environmental rights, and the right to environment, *Stanford Journal of International Law*, 28(103), pp. 103–138.

Sikka, P. (2011) Accounting for human rights: the challenge of globalization and foreign investment agreements, *Critical Perspectives on Accounting*, 22(8), pp. 811–827.

Sikka, P., Willmott, H. and Lowe, A. (1989) Guardians of knowledge and the public interest: evidence and issues of accountability in the UK accounting profession, *Accounting, Auditing & Accountability Journal*, 2(2), pp. 47–71.

Taylor, D. E. (2000). The rise of the environmental justice paradigm: injustice framing and the social construction of environmental discourses, *American Behavioral Scientist*, 43(4), pp. 508–580.

Taylor, M. B. (2011) The Ruggie framework: polycentric regulation and the implications for corporate social responsibility, *Etikk i praksis. Nordic Journal of Applied Ethics*, 5(1), pp. 9–30.

Tilbury, D., Stevenson, R. B., Fien, J. and Schreuder, D. (Eds) (2002) *Education and Sustainability: Responding to the Global Challenge* (Gland, Switzerland and Cambridge, UK, Commission on Education and Communication, IUCN).

Udombana, N. J. (2000) The third world and the right to development: agenda for the next millennium, *Human Rights Quarterly*, 22(3), pp. 753–787.

United Nations (1948) *Universal Declaration of Human Rights*. Available at http://www.un.org/en/documents/udhr/index.shtml

United Nations Human Rights, Office of the High Commissioner for Human Rights (n.d.) Special Representative of the Secretary-General on human rights and transnational corporations and other business enterprises. Available at http://www.ohchr.org/EN/Issues/Business/Pages/SRSGTransCorpIndex.aspx (accessed 7 August 2013).

United Nations Economic Commission for Europe (UNECE) (1999) Article 1.

Venkateswarlu, D. (2007) *Child Bondage Continues in Indian Cotton Supply Chain* (Hyderabad, India). Available at http://www.indianet.nl/pdf/childbondagecotton.pdf

Vischer, L. (2005) Human rights and sustainability: two conflicting notions? *Student World*, 1, pp. 47–58.

Walker, S. P. (1991) The defense of professional monopoly: Scottish chartered accountants and 'satellites in the accounting firmament' 1854–1914, *Accounting, Organizations and Society*, 16(3), pp. 257–283.

Walker, P. (1988) *The Society of Accountants in Edinburgh 1854–1914, A Study of Recruitment to a New Profession* (New York, USA: Garland Publishing).

Wettstein, F. (2010) The duty to protect: corporate complicity, political responsibility, and human rights advocacy, *Journal of Business Ethics*, 96, pp. 33–47.

Whelan, G., Moon, J. and Orlitzky, M. (2009) Human rights, transnational corporations and embedded liberalism: what chance consensus? *Journal of Business Ethics*, 87, pp. 367–383.

Wright, T. S. A. (2002) Definitions and frameworks for environmental sustainability in higher education, *International Journal of Sustainability in Higher Education*, 3(3), pp. 203–220.

Xstrata. (2009) *Sustainability Report*. Available at http://www.xstrata.com/content/assets/pdf/x_sustainability_2009.pdf (accessed 23 February 2011).

Zammit, A. (2003) *Development at Risk: Rethinking UN-Business Partnerships* (Geneva: South Centre and UNRISD).

such a challenge. For one, there currently are no hard, enforceable laws in the international arena preventing businesses from contributing to human rights violations, and without the rule of law compelling action on the part of business actors it seems wishful thinking to say that they are somewhat facing a threat. Moreover, such laws are not on the horizon, and one only needs to look at the opposition of powerful countries such as the USA to binding international agreements to see why business leaders might not be feeling particularly anxious about the issue of human rights, at least those whose businesses are not regularly scrutinized by non-governmental organizations (NGOs), the media, or social activists.[3]

The ongoing absence of the rule of law at the international level is and should be disconcerting, and even if human rights protections were legislated at this level, there would still be questions about whose values those 'protections' reflect (Sen, 1999). There would be concerns too about how to adequately define the transnational corporation or multinational enterprise so that it would be difficult for these entities to use financial and other devices to conceal their transnational nature (Weissbrodt and Kruger, 2003). Similarly, it would be difficult to establish how far along supply chains businesses must be concerned: should large MNCs be expected to monitor *all* of their contractors, subcontractors, suppliers, licensees, and other business partners (Weissbrodt and Kruger, 2003)?[4] More importantly, given the lapses in seemingly 'empowered' federal agencies like the Securities and Exchanges Commission (SEC) in the USA (cf. Arvedlund, 2009), it is unclear that the proper enforcement of regulations can even be carried out within countries, let alone across them.

Although the possibility of directly regulating the behaviour of global business actors is remote, there is hope. The source of that hope can be found in the market itself, which is ironic given business' role in the violation of human rights and environmental degradation. I am not referring here to the market for ethical or green products and services – though 'green marketing' has its merits (Peattie and Crane, 2005) – rather, I'm referring to the market for disclosure frameworks, 'transparency products' such as the United Nations' *Guiding Principles on Human Rights*, the Global Reporting Initiative (GRI), ISO 26000, and the OECD's *Principles of Corporate Governance* and *Guidelines on Multinational Enterprises*. It is from this symbolic market that business actors have been selecting their preferred frameworks and producing a variety of symbolic goods, all in the hopes of enhancing their corporate, if not personal, reputations.[5] This process has the potential to drive at least *small* changes in business practice and it has, consequently, resulted in more openness to the idea of practices such as corporate social responsibility (CSR) and environmental reporting.

For these disclosure systems to affect real change, however, I think they need to be transformed from soft into hard law, and this will mean mandating and enforcing these systems at the home-country level (Backer, 2008). As the author rightly points out, large multinational corporations have an immense amount of power on account of their economic capital. Another structural tension arises from their promotion of powerful ideologies, chief amongst which are shareholder wealth maximization and property (Backer, 2008). These ideologies have a long lineage, going back to the liberal political philosophies of figures like Smith, Locke, Mill, and, more recently, Friedman, von Hayek, and the Austrian School economists. One important theme to emerge from this work – and it must be said that the interpretations of some of these writers have been highly selective – is that individual rights and freedoms must be positioned above all other ideals. This includes rights and freedoms for corporations, which have, quite perversely, led the equating of money to speech and elections to bidding wars, as has become apparent in the USA following the Citizens United ruling and in the run-up to the 2012 US presidential election (Backer, 2008).

I think that the author needs to be more cognizant of the fact that the concern for human rights and the concern over shareholder wealth maximization and property are born of similar political philosophies. Both emanate from a 'quintessentially liberal program' (Walzer, 2002) that privileges the individual and universalizes its politics (Walzer, 2002; see also Everett and Friesen, 2010). This poses something of a problem for those wanting to prevent human rights abuses. With business' impetus to slash taxes and reshape laws and political processes in its favour, the business community can legitimately be viewed as simply exerting its 'individual free will and choice', or manifesting a form of moral agency that emanates from a set of presupposed, inalienable rights. It is for this reason that human rights discourse must be viewed as being more reformist than radical (Everett and Neu, 2000). When it lacks any backing in the rule of law or the state – that 'agency through which society acts back upon itself' (Walzer, 2002, p. 208) – its reformist potential becomes even more limited.

I would like to see the author move beyond calling for a business curriculum that remains rooted in what is, in effect, a morally individualist political philosophy. As an alternative, business curricula could start from a position that sees human actors not as atomistic 'centres of the universe', but as first and foremost moral actors born into a pre-existing world of humanity; a world, most importantly, not in which these actors so much exert 'moral choice', but one in which they have, a priori, a moral obligation to others (Walzer, 2002; Sandel, 2009). In such a world, responsibilities become just as important as rights.

I also think that the author's project would have been furthered by incorporating a perspective on information that explicitly views human rights and sustainability disclosures as conduits of power. On the one hand, and as is certainly the case under today's system of voluntary adoption, such disclosures, where they are not cynical attempts at blue- or green-washing, can be viewed as relatively benign artifacts designed only to convey information. Yet, they do much more: they also act as 'micro-capillaries' of power. As Foucault (1988) has shown us, 'calculative practices' – statistics, financial computations, budgets, and similar representational techniques – act as mediating mechanisms between those who govern and those who are governed. The external audiences of transnational corporations – those who govern – rely on calculations to enhance accountability and legitimacy, and their internal audiences depend upon calculations to enhance operations and discipline their members (Backer, 2012). It is because calculative practices are so important in mediating the relationship between the governed and those who govern that we have witnessed a veritable explosion of transparency systems, accountability indices and, more recently, experts equipped to monitor such systems. It is not surprising then that organizations have taken up the banner of transparency, recreating it when and where they are able, if not attempting to commodify transparency itself (Backer, 2012, p.106).

Business actors generally oppose state efforts to regulate their behaviour, yet they do accept the state's use of law to impose monitoring, reporting and disclosure requirements (Backer, 2008). Reporting and assurance, which are currently aimed at one primary set of constituents – shareholders and creditors – are now an accepted and taken-for-granted facet of corporate practice. It is here that human rights and sustainability advocates are presented with a means by which they can move corporate actors from a world wherein businesses aid and abet human rights violations to their envisioned world, wherein business actors employ their significant economic and symbolic power to prevent or remedy such violations.

There are now a host of voluntary CSR disclosure systems being promoted and used around the globe, and it seems unlikely that any one of them is going to be exclusively relied upon in the near term. On the one hand, this proliferation has been detrimental, as many businesses have based their choice of disclosure purely on cost, the potential to enhance reputation and legitimacy, or both. Moreover, adoption is still strictly voluntary, making enforcement moot and assurance largely symbolic.

Yet, the proliferation has also been beneficial, since it has enabled observers to learn about what works and what doesn't. They have learned, for instance, that voluntary codes work best 'when they produce standards that can be monitored, when they are embraced by companies willing to investigate stakeholder claims of violation, and when stakeholders can affect the consumer markets for companies irrespective of the existence of codes' (Backer, 2012, p. 142). They have also learned that legally enforceable monitoring systems can be substituted in the place of laws regulating actual behaviour, as we see in the case of securities law, and that compliance with information-gathering and reporting requirements and enforcement can be successfully vested at the nation-state level (Backer, 2008). Just as the enforcement of monitoring compliance regarding financial disclosures has been delegated to national securities agencies, the enforcement of monitoring compliance regarding CSR disclosures can be carried out at the nation-state level, either by independent civil society actors or state actors, which is to say that behavioural changes can be affected without having to rely on an international authority or strictly political actors. In effect, observers have learned that a focus on and mandating changes to 'calculative practices' enables the control of those who have the power to violate, protect, and/or remedy human rights and the natural environment. The key take-home is that securities regulators and those who establish and enforce corporate disclosure and monitoring requirements, on account of the impasse of the rule of law at the international level, should be viewed as potentially powerful actors in the struggle for human rights and environmental protection.

The author is correct in suggesting that greater literacy amongst business students regarding human rights and sustainability is needed, but the accounting classroom is only one of a number of venues where literacy needs to be enhanced. From my own experience, greater literacy also needs to be promoted in the economics and law courses that most business students are required to take. The current focus on neo-classical and macro-economics needs to be dramatically transformed and replaced with a more 'post-autistic' approach, one of which includes heterodox economics, feminist economics, green economics, values-based economics, socio-economics, and binary economics (Backer, 2008). Similarly, it is not enough to teach business students only the basics of civil and tort law, as new concerns in legal theory compel educators to teach students about enterprise liability, piercing-the-corporate-veil theories, extended jurisdictional theories, and extended notion of fiduciary duty (Backer, 2008).

Finally, I would agree with the author that business pedagogy must be critical, and not just in the sense of promoting the use of logic in argument, as many see the term, or in supporting critique that accepts accusation or that elevates rebellion into a value itself (Boltanski and Chiapello, 2005). Rather, it must be critical in the sense of promoting questions about the nature and legitimate use of power and authority, and, based on an in-depth examination of current facts, rather than just theoretical principles, whether the liberal project has actually made us 'free'. While the author doesn't provide any specific prescriptions regarding critical pedagogy, these should probably include a sustained consideration of the notion of commodification (Boltanski and Chiapello, 2005), what it means for transparency, or even human rights, to be commodified, and how accounting and its associated actors contribute to these processes. Motivating such critique embroils educators in debates over the role of the intellectual (Neu, Cooper and Everett, 2001) and, relevant to the author's call for incorporating human rights into the sustainability agenda, debates over social and environmental justice (Everett and Neu, 2000). In the end, all of these things must aim to enable students to become virtuous global actors, people of integrity and good judgement, who, if they are not actively seeking to reduce exploitation and injustice, are, at minimum, not contributing to them.

Notes

[1] See also Everett and Neu (2000), where the argument is made that the sustainability agenda should be more inclusive of social justice and human right concerns.

[2] By human rights, the author appears to have in mind two particular notions, the rights to environment and development (p. 396). This list could be expanded. Weissbrodt and Kruger (2003), for example, include: the right to equality of opportunity and treatment, the security of persons, the rights of workers, the right to collective bargaining, the respect for laws, a balanced approach to intellectual property rights, transparency and the avoidance of corruption, respect for the right to health, the freedom of movement, consumer protection, and environmental protection.

[3] This is not to say that change is not occurring. Small NGOs, some tiny, have had remarkable success in refocusing the attention of large corporations. The issue is whether business is currently facing a challenge.

[4] Consider that Proctor and Gamble's suppliers, for example, number in tens of thousands.

[5] Undoubtedly, many corporate leaders adopt these frameworks on account of a heartfelt need for change. There is little empirical evidence to suggest, however, that they are in the majority.

References

Arvedlund, E. (2009) *Too Good to Be True: The Rise and Fall of Bernie Madoff* (New York: Penguin).

Backer, L. C. (2008) From moral obligation to international law: disclosure systems, markets, and the regulation of multinational corporations, *Georgetown Journal of International Law*, 39, pp. 591–653.

Backer, L. C. (2012) Transparency and business in international law – governance between norm and technique, Working Paper No. 20123, Pennsylvania State University.

Boltanski, L. and Chiapello, E. (2005) The new spirit of capitalism, *International Journal of Politics, Culture, and Society*, 18(3), pp. 161–188.

Everett, J. and Friesen, C. (2010) Humanitarian accountability and performance in the Théâtre de l'Absurde, *Critical Perspectives on Accounting*, 21(6), pp. 468–485.

Everett, J. and Neu, D. (2000) Ecological modernization and the limits of environmental accounting?, *Accounting Forum*, 24(1), pp. 5–29.

Foucault, M. (1988) The political technology of individuals, in: *Technologies of the Self: A Seminar with Michel Foucault*, pp. 145–162 (London: Tavistock).

McPhail, K. (2013) Corporate responsibility to respect human rights and business schools' responsibility to teach it: incorporating human rights into the sustainability agenda, *Accounting Education: An International Journal*, 22(4), pp. 391–412.

Neu, D., Cooper, D. J. and Everett, J. (2001) Critical accounting interventions, *Critical Perspectives on Accounting*, 12(6), pp. 735–762.

Peattie, K. and Crane, A. (2005) Green marketing: legend, myth, farce or prophesy? *Qualitative Market Research: An International Journal*, 8(4), pp. 357–370.

Sandel, M. J. (2009) *Justice: What's the Right Thing to Do?* (New York: Farrar, Straus and Giroux).

Sen, A. (1999) *Development as Freedom* (Oxford: Oxford University Press).

Walzer, M. (2002) *The Company of Critics* (New York: Basic Books).

Weissbrodt, D. and Kruger, M. (2003) Norms on the responsibilities of transnational corporations and other busines enterprises with regards to human rights, *American Journal of International Law*, 97, pp. 901–922.

engage critically with the possibility that businesses (and accounting more specifically) may be able to support the realization of rights-related goals.

For human rights education to be taken seriously within business education, it is important that students are allowed to engage with complex issues. For example, McPhail (2013) discusses:

- the ideology of human rights (an acknowledgement that rights are deeply connected to politics, economics, culture, history and are 'constructed' rather than a natural order that has been interrupted by exploitative human endeavours);
- the role of the state (we are told they have a well-established responsibility for human rights despite the many well-documented abuses of rights that are perpetrated and/or obscured by governments);
- the growing importance of the multinational (as an economic and political power engaged in profit-making activity, as a contractor engaged to operationalize public policy, or as a multinational non-governmental organisation (NGO) pursuing a human rights initiative); and
- emergent global regulation (rewarding or enforcing human rights performance and encouraging broader disclosure of practices that have human rights implications).

In many ways the discussion within the paper models the kinds of discussions that we could have in our classrooms. Importantly, we learn that McPhail (2013) believes human rights education within a business degree should allow for discussion of ideals and that students are encouraged to see that practice is constructed and contested. This is an approach that creates space for students to formulate their own opinions and to imagine a future not as it already is, but one with alternate possibilities. In order to bring human rights into crowded business programmes, McPhail (2013) suggests that we see it as an extension of well-established sustainability discussions that already exist within most business schools and his paper offers us a variety of ways of thinking about this relationship and the connectedness that exists between these discourses. Again, one can only think that this produces excellent material for discussion within classrooms.

McPhail (2013) sets out to achieve two things: map the need for human rights education within business and accounting education; and challenge educators to extend the corporate social responsibility (CSR) literature to explore the connection between sustainability and human rights. He manages to do both. Although I am sympathetic to the aims of the paper, and agree whole-heartedly that a good business education would include a discussion of human rights, I was left wanting to know more about the role of accounting. Accounts produced by accountants for internal and external users remain a powerful tool, but offer only a limited path to decision-making and an even poorer proxy for accountability. From my perspective we need to educate a generation of 'critical' readers who are acutely aware of the partial nature of the information that supports decision-making. We also need to know more about the relationship between information and transformative action and what kinds of accounting may help to produce progressive social change that is sensitive to human rights; if, indeed, this is what we agree businesses, NGOs and governments should be doing.

We know that corporations are under pressure to improve their human rights records, they are watched by committed NGOs that report and expose poor performance, and they are becoming signatories to agreements, protocols, and guidance documents that require them to act in ways that respect human rights. Internally, a growing number of businesses are considering the impact that decisions have on human rights as part of their standard decision models. It would be naïve to suggest that this is because we are moving into an era of ethical capitalism, but it would also be inaccurate to argue that human rights will only be considered because of the economic consequences associated with breaching these obligations (whatever these may or may not be). The story must lie somewhere in between and the ill-defined nature of human rights in business practice provides wonderful classroom material for students to critique and debate. Importantly, as McPhail (2013) points out, our sustainability curriculum needs to be extended to encourage these kinds of discussions.

Reference

McPhail, K. (2013) Corporate responsibility to respect human rights and business schools' responsibility to teach it: incorporating human rights into the sustainability agenda, *Accounting Education: An International Journal*, 22(4), pp. 391–412.

While rights are of course ideological, I think it is important to point out that they are not necessarily connected to any singular ideology (see Dembour, 2006). I agree that we need to critically explore both the extent to which individualistic political philosophy underlines prevailing discussions of human rights and business, and the tension this understanding of rights may generate with communitarian views of sustainability. Levinas' work on rights and obligations, for example, may be helpful for critiquing the prevailing political rationality (see, for example, Burggraeve, 2005).

However, the idea of rights does not need to be based in liberalism or individualism. The distinction between individual and group rights, for example, is extensively discussed within the rights literature, with many contending that both are not incompatible (see, for example, Donnelly, 2003). The environmentalist literature has also explored the prospect of extending the idea of rights to natural objects. Stone (1972, p. 452, 456), for example, represents an early attempt at exploring the possibility of extending rights to trees and other natural objects.

The Rule of Law

Secondly, Everett (2013) is skeptical about the extent to which business schools are likely to embrace human rights because they are not legally enforceable. He comments (p. 414) that:

> there are no hard, enforceable laws in the international arena preventing businesses from contributing to human rights violations, and without the rule of law compelling action on the part of business actors it seems wishful thinking to say that they are somehow facing a threat.

The implication here is that human rights will only become an issue for business and business schools once the human rights responsibilities of corporations are codified in (inter)national law. However, a number of legal scholars suggest that new legal obligations are beginning to emerge (Cragg, Arnold and Muchlinski, 2012). While some attempts to extend human rights legislation to home-based companies have been unsuccessful (Cragg, Arnold and Muchlinski, 2012), there have been important developments. Lawyers continue to engaged in 'socially entrepreneurial public interest litigation' (Muchlinski, 2009), most notably drawing on provisions in the US Alien Torts Claims Act (ATCA). There is also new legislation in France and the Netherlands on parent company liability for human rights-related harms caused by overseas subsidiaries. Cragg, Arnold and Muchlinski (2012), and Section 1503 of the Dodd Frank Act in the USA, contain some disclosure requirements for companies in relation to operations in conflict zones. Muchlinski (2012) also concludes that the UN's *Framework* requirement that corporations exercise due diligence for the purpose of ensuring that they meet their responsibility to respect human rights will lead to the evolution of legally-binding duties under both national and international law.

Of course, as Everett (2013) rightly points out, given the way in which the law evolves there is no guarantee that it will necessarily serve the interests of the most vulnerable, whose rights are most likely to be violated. He says (p. 414):

> even if human rights protections were legislated at this level, there would still be questions about whose values those 'protections' reflect (Sen, 1999). There would be concerns too about how to adequately define the transnational corporation or multinational enterprise so that it would be difficult for these entities to use financial and other devices to conceal their transnational nature (Weissbrodt and Kruger, 2003).

I entirely agree, but my point isn't that these laws will necessarily be effective. Rather it is that as they take shape there will be a role for accounting and business academics in contributing towards their development. They will also have a role to play in analyzing their impact and engaging students in appraising their equity and effectiveness.

Everett (2013) concludes that the ideological basis of rights, combined with its lack of legal backing, means that we can expect the discourse of human rights to lead at most to reform rather than radical change. He concludes (p. 415):

> It is for this reason that human rights discourse must be viewed as more reformist than radical (Everett and Neu, 2000). When it lacks any backing in the rule of law or the state – that 'agency through which society acts back upon itself' (Walzer, 2002, p. 208) – its reformist potential becomes even more limited.

My own view, however, is that the idea of human rights is open for construction. It doesn't need to be reformist, because the idea of rights doesn't need to be connected solely to liberal individualism and its radical power does not need to depend entirely on legal backing. The American Civil Rights movement would at least provide a radical counter-example that might be worth exploring in contrast to the business and human rights agenda.

Professors Andrew (2013) and Everett (2013) raise some important concerns about the ideological underpinnings of the idea of rights and role of law in effecting change. These are real concerns that will require further critical analysis in the business school curriculum on business and human rights.

Conclusion and Recent Developments

What is certain is that the issue of business and human rights is a major development in global governance. It is a fast-evolving field that I anticipate will continue to grow in significance and importance. In the short time between writing the paper and replying to the Commentaries, a number of significant developments have taken place within the field. For example, The United Nations (UN) held its first annual forum on business and human rights in December 2012 in Geneva, at which various developments were discussed. For example, European Union (EU) member states are developing national plans of action on business and human rights. The UK published its plan at the beginning of 2013. The EU has also published a guide to human rights for small- and medium-sized enterprises (SMEs), based on the *Guiding Principles* (Ruggie, 2013). Mezars, along with SHIFT, are also involved in a project to develop an international standard on human rights audit. It was suggested that one of the problems of integrating the *Guiding Principles* into the business sphere was the lack of practitioners with human rights experience within the business community (Ruggie, 2013). The recurring themes at the forum of emerging policy developments and the lack of capacity within the business community to implement those policies underlines the argument that business schools should incorporate a critical understanding of business and human rights into the business school curriculum.

The UN's *Global Compact Principles of Responsible Management* (PRIME) initiative is currently in the process of establishing a working group on business and human rights, while the *Journal of Business Ethics Education* will soon release a call for a special issue on capacity building in business and human rights. Please get in touch if you would like to know more about either of these developments.

References

Andrew, J. (2013) Incorporating human rights into the sustainability agenda, *Accounting Education: An International Journal*, 22(4), pp. 418–420.

Burggraeve, R. (2005) The good and its shadow: the view of Levinas on human rights as the surpassing of political rationality, *Human Rights Review*, 6(2), pp. 80–101.

Cragg, W., Arnold, D. and Muchlinski, P. (2012) Human rights and business, *Business Ethics Quarterly*, 1(22), pp. 1–7.

Dembour, M. B. (2006) *Who Believes in Human Rights: Reflections on the European Convention* (Cambridge: Cambridge University Press).

Donnelly, J. (2003) *Universal Human Rights in Theory and Practice* (Cornell: Cornell University Press).

Everett, J. (2013) A commentary on 'Corporate responsibility to respect human rights and business schools' responsibility to teach it', *Accounting Education: An International Journal*, 22(4), pp. 413–417.

Everett, J. and Friesen, C. (2010) Humanitarian accountability and performance in the Théâtre de l'Absurde, *Critical Perspectives on Accounting*, 21(6), pp. 468–485.

Everett, J. and Neu, D. (2000) Ecological modernization and the limits of environmental accounting? *Accounting Forum*, 24(1), pp. 5–29.

McPhail, K. (2013) Corporate responsibility to respect human rights and business schools' responsibility to teach it: incorporating human rights into the sustainability agenda, *Accounting Education: An International Journal*, 22(4), pp. 391–412.

Muchlinski, P. (2009) The provision of private law remedies against multinational enterprises: a comparative law perspective, *Journal of Comparative Law*, 4(2), pp. 148–70.

Muchlinski, P. (2012) Implementing the new UN corporate human rights framework: implications for corporate law, governance, and regulation, *Business Ethics Quarterly*, 22(1), pp. 145–77.

Ruggie, J. (2013) *Summary of Discussions of the Forum on Business and Human Rights, Prepared by the Chairperson, John Ruggie, United Nations Human Rights Council, Forum on Business and Human Rights*, first session 4–5 December 2012, A /HRC/FBHR/2012/4. Available at http://www.ohchr.org/Documents/Issues/Business/ForumSession1/A_HRC_FBHR_2012_4_en.pdf

Sen, A. (1999) *Development as Freedom* (Oxford: Oxford University Press).

Stone, D (1972) Should trees have standing? Toward legal rights for natural objects, *Southern Californian Law Review*, 45, pp. 450–502.

Walzer, M. (2002) *The Company of Critics* (New York: Basic Books).

Index

www.routledge.com/9780415699204

Related titles from Routledge

Personal Transferable Skills in Accounting Education

Edited by Kim Watty, Beverley Jackling and Richard M. S. Wilson

The development of generic skills (often referred to as 'soft skills') in accounting education has been a focus of discussion and debate for several decades. During this time employers and professional bodies have urged accounting educators to consider and develop curricula which provide for the development and assessment of these skills. In addition, there has been criticism of the quality of accounting graduates and their ability to operate effectively in a global economy. Embedding generic skills in the accounting curriculum has been acknowledged as an appropriate means of addressing the need to provide 'knowledge professionals' to meet the needs of a global business environment.

This book was originally published as a special issue of *Accounting Education: an international journal.*

January 2012: 246 x 174: 192pp
Hb: 978-0-415-69920-4
£85 / $145

For more information and to order a copy visit
www.routledge.com/9780415699204

Available from all good bookshops